RAND NATIONAL SECURITY RESEARCH DIVISION

D1711458

The Defender's Dilemma

Charting a Course Toward Cybersecurity

Martin C. Libicki, Lillian Ablon, Tim Webb

Prepared for Juniper Networks, Inc.

For more information on this publication, visit www.rand.org/t/rr1024

Library of Congress Cataloging-in-Publication Data
ISBN: 9780833089113

Published by the RAND Corporation, Santa Monica, Calif.
© Copyright 2015 RAND Corporation
RAND® is a registered trademark.

Support RAND
Make a tax-deductible charitable contribution at
www.rand.org/giving/contribute

www.rand.org

Preface

Cybersecurity is a constant and, by all accounts, growing challenge. Although software products are gradually becoming more secure and novel approaches to cybersecurity are being developed, hackers are becoming more adept and better equipped. Their markets are flourishing and the value at stake is growing. The rising tide of network intrusions has focused organizations' attention on how to protect themselves better. But some are now asking how much longer today's approach to cybersecurity will remain viable before something radically new will be needed.

To address these concerns, RAND conducted a multiphased study of the future of cybersecurity, under the sponsorship of Juniper Networks. The first report, *Markets for Cybercrime Tools and Stolen Data: Hackers' Bazaar*, examined cybercrime markets. This report scopes the future of cybersecurity by interviewing chief information security officers, taking a deep dive into the burgeoning world of cybersecurity products, and reviewing the relationship between software quality and vulnerability discovery processes. Insights from these three components (interviews, cybersecurity products, and vulnerability discovery trends) were used to develop a heuristic model that can shed light on the relationship between organizational choices and the cost of confronting cyberattacks.

This report should be of interest to the cybersecurity and information security communities.

The research was conducted within the Acquisition and Technology Policy (ATP) Center of the RAND National Security Research

Division (NSRD). NSRD conducts research and analysis on defense and national security topics for the U.S. and allied defense, foreign policy, homeland security, and intelligence communities and foundations and other nongovernmental organizations that support defense and national security analysis.

For more information on the ATP Center, see http://www.rand.org/nsrd/ndri/centers/atp.html or contact the director (contact information is provided on the web page).

Contents

Figures

Tables

Summary

Cybersecurity is, in part, a world of secrecy. Organizations charged with protecting information from disclosure are understandably prone to concealing at least some of the practices used to hide that information. Further, the world of cybersecurity suffers from short-sighted analysis: There is great debate about what malefactors are doing to networks, but less discussion about the short- or long-term effects of this activity. Malicious hackers, whose success requires subverting computers, are certainly not putting out statistics on their activity. Moreover, surprise is endemic to cyberattack.[1] Compromising an assiduously defended system or network (or subverting diligently written software) is often accomplished by finding a path in that has eluded the attention of those charged with keeping such paths closed. Since defenders rarely let known holes go unpatched for very long,[2] the success of a hacker often depends on finding an unknown (or at least unwatched) hole—tantamount to a surprise.

Thus, there is a great and urgent need to understand the evolution of the cybersecurity space. The Gartner research firm estimates that worldwide spending on cybersecurity is approaching $70 billion per year (Giles, 2014) and is growing at roughly 10 to 15 percent annu-

---

[1] The use of the term *cyberattack* in this report encompasses the traditional definition of the word, as well as the current media use of the word—i.e., affecting an entity's network to attack in the traditional sense (disrupt, deny, degrade, destroy, or deceive); conduct intelligence, surveillance, and/or reconnaissance; and exploit or exfiltrate data or information.

[2] This statement takes into account systems that work around the clock and thus cannot be taken down easily for maintenance.

ally with no deceleration in sight. Despite this, it would be an understatement to say that organizations are dissatisfied with existing cybersecurity—and there is scant confidence among defenders that their exertions will give them the upper hand against malicious hackers two to five years out. Many believe that hackers are gaining on defenders. This combination of rising expenditures and questionable success creates a sense that security efforts cannot continue on this course.

Our purpose in this report is to understand the fundamental forces driving cybersecurity. To this end, we have interviewed chief information security officers (CISOs), reviewed the cybersecurity industry's slate of cutting-edge products, and assessed the struggles of the software industry (and its foes) to make or (alternatively) break secure software. With this background, we used heuristic modeling to illustrate how some of these forces might interact with one another. We conclude with some lessons for organizations and public policymakers on how to promote cybersecurity in a cost-effective manner.

In doing so, we bring several assumptions into play.

First, the proper goal of a cybersecurity program (or policy) is to minimize the combined cost of expenditures on cybersecurity plus the expected costs arising from cyberattacks (e.g., network or facility down-time, costs of recovery, loss of reputation). This is difficult to measure, however. Organizations can measure what they spend on cybersecurity but can only guess at the costs their security measures have saved, for a couple of reasons. Not only is it difficult to prove a negative (an attack prevented), but many of these costs can be tricky to calculate—notably the often-mentioned impact of a potential cyberattack on an organization's reputation.[3]

Second, malicious hackers are also sensitive to costs and benefits, and they understand how to respond to market signals (Ablon, Libicki, and Golay, 2014). They weigh the relationship between the effort associated with penetrating and exploiting a system and the gains from doing so—gains that, incidentally, are generally much lower than the costs to the organization that has been hacked. The harder a system is to infiltrate,

---

[3]   There are those, however, who aim to summarize the costs. Ponemon Institute (2013a), for example, puts out a report each year on the average cost of a data breach.

the more effort hackers must put into cracking it; for some systems, such efforts may be deemed unprofitable. Similarly, if systems were harder to crack, fewer hackers would be capable of breaking into them, and those who could might have other priorities. But for an organization defending itself against a state intelligence apparatus determined to access it, a system has to get fairly close to being impenetrable to be secure.

Third, although cyberattacks vary greatly, many of them, particularly those associated with advanced persistent threats, tend to have two important stages. One is achieved when attackers penetrate client systems (e.g., computers of end users). The other is achieved when attackers leverage the penetration of client systems to move throughout the victim network and compromise their target. Keeping hackers from penetrating client systems depends on a multitude of factors, but attention can be given to the quality of software on the client systems themselves (e.g., web browser add-ons). Keeping penetrated client systems from compromising the network may be a matter of adroitly administered software and/or services that implement a security watch over the entire system.

Fourth, because malicious hackers are thinking adversaries, many measures to improve security beget countermeasures. The extent to which these countermeasures negate all, some, or none of the initial measures' improvements can vary greatly. We concentrate on two measure-countermeasure contests. The first focuses on investments made in tools to discern the activities of hackers within organizations contrasted with the techniques that hackers use to operate below the visibility of such tools. The other contest deals with efforts to reduce the exploitable faults in the software stack and how those measure up to the tools and techniques used by hackers to find and exploit such faults (although some hackers do wear white hats in this case, enough wear black hats to ensure this contest is no game).

Findings

As a result of interviewing 18 CISOs, we drew three sets of conclusions: those we expected, those that confirmed our suppositions, and those that came as surprises.

The conclusions we expected were as follows:

- Security postures are highly specific to company type, size, etc., and there often are not good solutions for smaller businesses.
- The importance of intellectual property varies with the individual firms' missions.
- Cybersecurity is a hard sell, especially to chief executives.
- Although CISOs generally lack a way to know whether they are spending enough on cybersecurity, they split between those who think spending is sufficient and those who feel more is needed.
- Air-gapping, wherein networks are electronically isolated from the Internet, can be a useful option. (In a softer form, it is compatible with tunneling through the Internet but otherwise not interacting with it).
- Responding to the desire of employees to bring their own devices (BYOD) and connect them to the network creates growing dilemmas.
- CISOs feel that attackers have the upper hand, and will continue to have it.

The conclusions that confirmed our suspicions were these:

- Customers look to extant tools for solutions even though they do not necessarily know what they need and are certain no magic wand exists.
- When given more money for cybersecurity, a majority of CISOs choose human-centric solutions.
- CISOs want information on the motives and methods of specific attackers, but there is no consensus on how such information could be used.
- Current cyberinsurance offerings are often seen as more hassle than benefit, useful in only specific scenarios, and providing little return.
- The concept of *active defense* has multiple meanings, no standard definition, and evokes little enthusiasm.
- CISOs lack a clear vision on incentives.

- Information-sharing tends to live within a web of trust.
- CISOs tend to be optimistic about the cloud, but, apart from those who sell cloud services, most are willing to be only cautious fast followers.
- CISOs are likely to assign lower priority to security-as-a-service offerings.
- CISOs, in general, are not ready to concentrate their purchases from a single vendor (but also are not sure that heterogeneity is the best solution, either).

The conclusions that came as surprises were the following:

- A cyberattack's effect on reputation (rather than more-direct costs) is the biggest cause of concern for CISOs. The actual intellectual property or data that might be affected matters less than the fact that *any* intellectual property or data are at risk.
- In general, loss estimation processes are not particularly comprehensive.
- The ability to understand and articulate an organization's risk arising from network penetrations in a standard and consistent matter does not exist and will not exist for a long time.

The contest between measures (new security capabilities) and countermeasures (attempts to undermine those capabilities) is escalating and has been evolving for quite some time. To take just one example, basic firewall filtering yielded to finer-grain signature-based examination with intrusion detection and prevention systems and deep packet inspection. As companies learned that they needed to reduce not only the likelihood but also the impact of attacks, they turned to data loss prevention (DLP) programs and more-expansive use of virtual private networks (VPNs). Attackers, in turn, made more use of stealth, obfuscation, and malware polymorphism. Defenders shifted to detecting attacks based on network behaviors and not signatures. Sometimes the same tools and techniques were used by both defenders and attackers. As the novelty and innovation of each new technique was met with new countermeasures, it became harder to distinguish those that worked well from those that were merely added complexity and noise, thereby taxing an organization's limited time and resources. Without metrics, it is unclear why consumers would pay more for good products over merely adequate ones. And the best tools and largest resources could not get around the many security weaknesses that arose from human nature.

If network and software architectures were static, defenders would eventually gain the upper hand—but innovation is the lifeblood of the information technology sector. Similarly, if networks were inherently harder, systematic progress might be made toward security. "Walled garden" software systems (where the provider controls all aspects of content and transactions) have generally proven more difficult to attack than open systems. But the trend over the past 20 years has been in the other direction—greater reliance on open systems for both software and networking.

The bedrock of cybersecurity is good system software. Companies often find themselves having to invest in defensive measures because foundational systems and software are unsecure. The security and solidness of the actual software helps to prevent attackers from gaining a foothold on a network (what we call the *external hardness* of an organization). But once they are in, additional defenses are then required to prevent attackers from converting that foothold into something that hurts the organization (what we call the *internal hardness* of an organization). As it is, software vulnerabilities and weaknesses arise through design (architectural) or implementation (coding) faults. A subset of these vulnerabilities is *exploitable*, in that an attacker can perform some sort of unintended action with the ultimate goal being remote code execution (giving an actor full control over a target's system). Sometimes, these software vulnerabilities are found and fixed before release. Other times, the vendor discovers the vulnerabilities after customers have the product and provides patches. Still other times, researchers not tied to the vendor can discover these (zero-day) vulnerabilities;[4] when they do, their options include informing the vendor (white markets), selling the information to

---

[4] A *zero-day vulnerability* is one for which no patch has been developed (usually because the vendor of the software is unaware that the software has that particular vulnerability).

governments or their suppliers (gray markets), or selling the information to cybercriminals (black markets). Because finding the vulnerabilities is nontrivial, doing so can fetch a great deal of money. Unfortunately, fixing such vulnerabilities often introduces new problems—and even when it does not, malware and attacks spike after disclosure of these vulnerabilities and even after the release of a corresponding patch.

However, software design trends indicate that there might one day be enough improvement to raise questions about the assumption that attackers have to be defeated within the network (minimizing damage) rather than before they get into the network (preventing damage). The three most frequently used Internet browsers (Internet Explorer, Firefox, and Chrome) are evolving to where corrupted web pages create faults that propagate only within the browser rather than the operating system. Further, operating systems and browsers themselves are improving (in large part because patching has become more automated) and require increasingly sophisticated campaigns to infect.

Conversely, there are burgeoning sets of network relationships arising from the Internet of Things (IoT) and from the many privileges that organizations conclude they must extend to other organizations.[5] These make the perimeter harder to identify, thus harder to guard, and means that cybersecurity efforts must be based on the assumption that bad guys are already in the network and that security has to be managed even more intensively at the systemic level, rather than focusing on keeping attackers out of a system in the first place.

We used the results of our analysis to construct a heuristic model for cybersecurity as a way of framing the problem and allowing some systematic treatment of its underlying factors. We drew our basic variables from all three aspects of our research, paying particular attention to the concerns and the methods used by CISOs and the measure-countermeasure struggles.

---

[5] *Internet of Things* refers to a near future when every electronic or even electrical device (e.g., a microwave oven) is connected to the Internet.

Our model portrays the struggle of organizations to minimize the cost arising from insecurity in cyberspace (over a ten-year period). Those costs are defined as the sum of

- losses from cyberattack
- direct costs of training users
- direct cost of buying and using tools
- indirect costs associated with restrictions on the ingestion of BYOD/smart devices
- indirect costs of air-gapping particularly sensitive subnetworks.

Calculations were carried out for year 0 (assume it to be 2015) and iterated for each year over a subsequent ten-year period. Changes over time include the number and vulnerability of computers and devices, shifts in the losses associated with cyberattacks, the introduction of new tools, and the declining efficacy of some tools in the face of countermeasures. The odds that an organization was successfully attacked in a given year were deemed to be a product of an organization's external hardness (its ability to keep attackers from establishing a beachhead within an organization's network) and internal hardness (its ability to keep a beachhead from being converted into a systemic compromise). Its projected losses from cyberattack were the product of those odds of successful attack multiplied by value at risk. In other words, hardness, both external and internal, can be considered as a probabilistic measure. When both external and internal hardness equal 0, an attack is absolutely likely to penetrate an organization, and a penetration is absolutely likely to lead to compromise and hence loss of value at risk. If *either* external hardness *or* internal hardness is 1, either an attack will be stopped at the border or no form of penetration will result in a compromised system.

The model runs five subroutines in a specific order to determine an organization's possible losses from cyberattack. These subroutines represent parameters discussed by CISOs. They are run in sequence, rather than in parallel, to represent a progression from hope to painful commitment:

- We hope that training users suffices.

- If that does not work well enough, we buy cybersecurity tools to thwart attackers.
- If the combination of training and tools does not prove sufficient, we work on restrictions: first, to head off the burgeoning increases in addressable devices; second, to ensure that at least the most critical processes are protected through isolation.

Each affects one of the three parameters: external hardness, internal hardness, and value at risk.

- First, the odds that every computer and smart device (something as intelligent as, but not used as, a computer in the traditional sense) can repel an attacker are calculated based on the number of computers and devices and the quality of their software. This determines an organization's initial external hardness.
- Second, an organization can improve its external hardness by increasing the level of training (think also of restrictions on users' ability to make changes to their own machines and/or access organizational assets).
- Third, an organization's internal hardness is enhanced to the extent that it buys cybersecurity tools.[6]
- Fourth, an organization can increase external hardness by successively reducing the number of connected devices it supports, in large part by restricting what employees can bring into the network (as a practical matter, other policy tools are also available, including those that determine which devices are visible to the outside).
- Fifth, an organization can reduce the cost of a cyberattack by isolating parts of its networks where compromise might be particularly costly.

The model yields a plethora of results, of which the following merit note:

---

[6] In practice, companies have to use these tools intelligently, and many do not. An attribute applied to organizations, diligence, captures the difference between those who use cybersecurity tools well and those who do not.

- The various instruments that organizations can use to control the losses from cyberattack are collectively powerful. Yet much of what they do is to transfer costs from losses to defenses: Roughly one-third of the reduced losses are offset by increased costs associated with using such instruments (direct acquisition and usage costs plus implicit reduction in the value of networking). Developing instruments that offer better cost-effectiveness ratios would be important.
- The size of the organization matters greatly to its optimal strategy. Small organizations benefit from circumstances and policies that reduce their attack surface (e.g., BYOD/smart device policies). Larger organizations need a panoply of instruments to keep costs under control. One size does not fit all.
- The quality of software used by organizations is an important exogenous factor in determining their susceptibility to penetration. There need to be better mechanisms to convey the interests that organizations have in the quality of code to those responsible for getting the code into products.
- Over time, the potential influence of devices on cybersecurity will approach and perhaps exceed the influence of computers on cybersecurity. The introduction of networked computers into organization in the 1980s and 1990s was allowed to happen without a very sophisticated understanding of the security implications. The same mistake ought not be made with intelligent devices.
- Tools that do not lend themselves to countermeasures (e.g., better configuration management) are likely to retain their usefulness in the long run. By year 10, of the top dozen tools (out of 30), only one was a tool of the sort that could be subject to countermeasures (and that was a tool introduced in the last year of the model). If measures are taken to increase the number of tools available to organizations—which, as the model suggests, can cut losses substantially—then the choice of such tools should take the slower obsolescence of such tools in mind (vis-à-vis, for instance, those that seek to differentiate the signal of attack from the noise of background).

Organizational and Policy Lessons

Our research leads us to draw one set of lessons for organizations and a separate set for policymakers.

Organizational Lessons

- **Know what needs protecting, and how badly protection is needed.** Part of self-knowledge is understanding what is worth protecting; in that regard, it was striking how frequently a corporation's reputation was widely cited by CISOs as a prime cause for cybersecurity spending. Another part is knowing what machines are on the network, what applications they are running, what privileges have been established, and with what state of security. The advent of the IoT (smart phones, tablets, and so forth) compounds the problem.
- **Know where to devote effort to protect the organization.** A core choice for companies is how much defense to commit to the perimeter and how much to internal workings. Attackers often establish a persistent presence in networks when an employee opens a bad attachment or goes to a malicious website. Once penetrated, weaknesses in other code enable the malicious code either to execute its own instructions or obey those of the attacker. Better code would make this process much more difficult. But infections are possible even with better code, so multiple tools must be employed.
- **Consider the potential for adversaries to employ countermeasures.** Mounting a defense is a necessary first step. But as defenses are installed, organizations must realize they are dealing with a thinking adversary and that measures installed to thwart hackers tend to induce countermeasures as hackers probe for ways around or through new defenses. This tit-for-tat exchange will eventually drive measures toward increasing expense, additional complexity, and, arguably, less reliability. Corporations should think about installing measures of the sort that are less likely to attract countermeasures.

Policy Lessons

By and large, CISOs we interviewed did not express much interest in government efforts to improve cybersecurity, other than a willingness to cooperate after an attack. Yet it seems likely that government should be able to play a useful role. The question is what sort of role would be mutually beneficial and perceived as such. One option is to build a body of knowledge on how systems fail (a necessary prerequisite to preventing failure) and then share that information. The government plays a similar role in the aviation and medical fields. A community that is prepared to share what went wrong and what could be done better next time could collectively educate the world's CISOs and produce higher levels of cybersecurity.

Conclusions

One conclusion is a seeming paradox: The amount of pessimism expressed over cybersecurity is cause for hope. One result of this dour view is that CISOs are both more numerous and more influential than they were five years ago, let alone ten. Core software is improving, and cybersecurity products are burgeoning. The combination is likely to make the attacker's task more difficult and more expensive—which will not solve the problem, but will make it more manageable.

Hurdles remain, of course. Our earlier work, *Markets for Cybercrime Tools and Stolen Data: Hackers' Bazaar,* pointed out that hackers who knew how to infiltrate networks but not how to take criminal advantage of that infiltration are now trading expertise with those who do. This union makes the business of hacking more profitable—and, thus, more attractive. Second, the IoT might provide hackers with many more pathways to exploit. Still, while the challenges are formidable, they are not insurmountable, and those who defend networks are engaged fully.

Acknowledgments

RAND reports typically draw on a wide collection of supporters, collaborators, and helpers in their creation. We would first like to mention the invaluable insights provided by the numerous experts at Juniper Networks and Edelman Corporation. Within RAND, Cynthia Cook and Henry Willis have been wise and patient in their assistance and insight to this project. Our reviewers, Herb Lin and Bradley Wilson, offered sage advice that improved the report.

Finally, we are exceptionally grateful to the 18 chief information security officers and the numerous bug bounty directors, zero-day market vendors, and other computer security professionals who took the time to share their insights and provide their input on the cybersecurity landscape.

Abbreviations

API	application portability interfaces
APT	advanced persistent threat
ASLR	address space layout randomization
BYOD	bring your own device
CEO	chief executive officer
CISO	chief information security officer
DDoS	distributed denial of service
DEP	data execution prevention
DLP	data loss prevention
EMET	Enhanced Mitigation Experience Toolkit
FTP	file transfer protocol
IDS	intrusion detection system
IoT	internet of things
NNTP	network news transfer protocol
POC	proof of concept
RCX	remote code execution
ROP	return-oriented programming
SMTP	simple mail transfer protocol
ZDI	zero-day initiative

CHAPTER ONE

Introduction

Delving into the future of security in cyberspace would seem a fool's errand. Cybersecurity is a world of secrecy, where there is great dispute about what malefactors are *currently* doing to networks but very little focus on the effects of such activity. Organizations charged with protecting information from disclosure are understandably prone to concealing at least some of the practices used to hide that information. Malicious hackers, whose success requires subverting computers, are certainly not putting out statistics on their activity. High levels of classification characterize both offensive and defensive operations within all governments, not just the U.S. government. Further, surprise is endemic to cyberattack.

Compromising an assiduously defended system or network (or subverting diligently written software) is often accomplished by finding a path in that has eluded the attention of those charged with keeping such paths closed. Since defenders rarely let known holes go unpatched for very long,[1] the success of a hacker often depends on finding an unknown (or at least unwatched) hole—tantamount to a surprise.

Nevertheless, there is a great and urgent need to understand the evolution of the cybersecurity space. The Gartner research firm estimates that worldwide spending on cybersecurity is approaching $70 billion per year (Giles, 2014), and growing at roughly 10 to 15 percent annually with no deceleration in sight. And yet, it would be an understatement to say organizations are dissatisfied with their security.

---

[1] This statement takes into account systems that work around the clock and thus cannot be taken down easily for maintenance.

There is scant confidence among defenders that their current exertions will give them the upper hand against malicious hackers two to five years from now. Many believe the hackers are gaining on defenders. The combination of rising expenditures and questionable results creates a sense that security efforts cannot continue on this course.

Our purpose in writing this report is to explain the fundamental forces driving cybersecurity. We interviewed chief information security officers (CISOs), reviewed the slate of products that have been or are being introduced by the cybersecurity industry, and assessed the struggles of the software industry (and its foes) to make or (alternatively) break secure software. With this background, we used heuristic modeling to illustrate how some of these forces might interact. We conclude with some lessons for organizations and public policy that would promote cybersecurity in a cost-effective manner.

In doing so, we bring several assumptions into play.

First, the proper goal of a cybersecurity program (or policy) is to minimize the combined cost of expenditures on cybersecurity and the expected costs arising from cyberattacks. An organization that is spending a dollar to save 99 cents is probably not working in its own best interests; the same goes for one that refuses to spend 99 cents to save a dollar in costs. In practice, this is difficult to measure. Organizations know what they spend on cybersecurity but can only guess what costs they have saved through their security measures. Not only is it difficult to prove a negative (an attack prevented), but many of these costs can be tricky to calculate—notably the often-mentioned impact of a potential cyberattack on an organization's reputation.[2]

Second, malicious hackers are also sensitive to costs and benefits and understand how to respond to market signals (Ablon, Libicki, and Golay, 2014). They weigh the relationship between the effort associated with penetrating and exploiting a system and the gains from doing so—gains that, incidentally, are generally much lower than the costs

---

[2]   There are those, however, who aim to summarize the costs. Ponemon Institute, for example, puts out a report each year on the average cost of a data breach (Ponemon, 2013a). It might be the difficulty of accurately measuring the specific costs arising from hacking that leads CISOs to lean on reputation as the primary way that their organizations might be hurt by cyberattacks.

to the organization that has been hacked. The harder a system is to infiltrate, the more effort hackers must put into cracking it; for some systems, such efforts might be deemed unprofitable. Similarly, if systems were harder to crack, fewer hackers would be capable of breaking into them, and those who could might have other priorities. Thus, an organization does not necessarily have to make itself impenetrable to reduce attention from those potentially capable of cracking it.[3] But for an organization defending itself against a state intelligence apparatus determined to access it, a system has to get fairly close to impenetrability to be secure.

Third, although cyberattacks vary greatly, many of them, particularly those associated with advanced persistent threats, tend to have two important stages. The first stage is when attackers penetrate client systems (e.g., computers of end users). The second stage is when attackers leverage the penetration of client systems to move throughout the victim network and accomplish their ultimate goal (e.g., removing personal financial information or intellectual property). Keeping hackers from penetrating client systems depends on a multitude of factors, but attention can be given to the quality of software on the client systems themselves. (For example, if a corrupted PDF permitted the breach, was the exploit a zero-day and/or a patched vulnerability whose patch was not installed?)[4] Keeping penetrated client systems from ultimately damaging an organization might be a matter of adroitly administered software and/or services that implement a security watch over the system itself.

---

[3] The old saw goes that safety consists not of running faster than the bear, but of running faster than others also running away from the bear. It is unclear how applicable this in cyberspace, but in a world where a fixed number of hackers try every door and keep working only if the door budges, being safer than everyone else is important. Resulting reputation is also relative: Being hacked along with everyone else is less likely to make one an outlier, but avoiding it rates a gold star. However, a number of hackers respond to absolute rewards, so a relatively hard target might still attract those who will try to get in as long as they believe their efforts will net worthwhile results.

[4] A *zero-day vulnerability* is one for which no patch has been developed (usually because the vendor of the software is unaware that the software has that particular vulnerability).

Fourth, because malicious hackers are thinking adversaries, many measures to improve security beget countermeasures. The extent to which these countermeasures negate all, some, or none of the improvements arising from the initial measures' improvements can vary greatly. An earlier RAND report (Ablon, Libicki, and Golay, 2014) illustrated that as hackers develop tools and techniques to carry out exchanges beyond the purview of the law, law enforcement officials develop tools and techniques to discern what the hackers are up to. In this report, we concentrate on two measure-countermeasure contests. One deals with the efforts to reduce the exploitable faults in the software stack and how those measure up to the tools and techniques used by hackers to find and exploits such faults. (Admittedly, some hackers wear white hats, but enough of them wear black hats to ensure that this contest is no game.) The other focuses on investments made in tools to discern the activities of hackers within organizations contrasted with the techniques that hackers use to operate below the visibility of such tools. Often the same tool (e.g., Metasploit) can be used by both sides.

Organization of This Report

Chapter Two is built from interviews with 18 chief information system officers (CISOs) or their equivalents. We wanted to understand the extent to which they believed that the cybersecurity tools available were adequate to the challenge or if they were on the lookout for something radically different. To shed light on this question, we developed a 21-item questionnaire (see Chapter Two and Appendix A) and administered it through a series of one-on-one telephone conversations, generally lasting from 45 to 60 minutes.[5] Because of the normal difficulty of getting CISOs to talk to those they do not know personally, the number of interviews and the randomness of the sample are both below what would be required to draw reliable statistical inferences. Nevertheless, the insights available from the interviews were useful in generating elements of the heuristic model; particularly the use of such

---

[5]   In two cases, email answers were provided instead.

techniques as training, tools, controls over employee-owned devices, and air-gapping (wherein networks are electronically isolated from the Internet)[6]—the four main characteristics of an organization's exposure to risk that an organization or CISO can influence. These four characteristics (run as subroutines in the model) have direct cost implications associated with preventing cyberattacks. Chapter Two lays out useful findings from these conversations.

Chapter Three examines the contest between the techniques that organizations are using to defend their systems and the countermeasures that are currently and might soon be used to evade such measures. Lockheed Martin's "cyber kill chain" (Lockheed Martin, 2014), for instance, attempts to understand the six tasks that an attacker must complete to extract value, and thus provides many ways to hinder the attacker's progress. Correspondingly, many of these measures on the market involve looking for anomalies in network performance. Others gather intelligence on potential attackers and use this information to create signatures of their activity that can be used by intrusion detection/prevention systems. Many of the new techniques are being developed by start-ups dedicated to this purpose, but they are also within the repertoire of established vendors. This chapter builds the foundation for many of the model's parameters, particularly those associated with tools and air-gapping. Tools are the key components in the measure-countermeasure game, and essential for determining the extent to which a penetration can lead to a system compromise (referred to as *internal hardness* in the model).

Chapter Four examines the contest between software writers and those looking for exploitable vulnerabilities in the software. Some of the contest is entirely white-hat in that those looking for vulnerabilities fully intend to inform vendors of the mistakes they need to fix (some for free, others for reward)—but some gray-market and black-market researchers are developing ways to exploit these faults. Understandably, there is a substantial difference between theoretical exploits dreamed up by researchers and those used by attackers. Builders of operating

---

[6]   In a softer form, air-gapping is compatible with tunneling through the Internet but otherwise not interacting with it.

systems and web browsers are developing exploitation mitigation techniques, such as browser sandboxing and address-space layout randomization (ASLR), to prevent application vulnerabilities being converted into opportunities for remote code execution (RCX).[7]

Thus, when going against modern software (which, admittedly, is not representative of a typical organization's entire attack surface), hackers have to chain together several exploits to succeed. This chapter builds other elements of the model's parameters—namely, those associated with training and with employees who bring their own devices (BYOD) and connect them to the network—and key elements of an organization's an organization's ability to repel cyberattacks from the outside, or *external hardness*. Additionally, the model distinguishes between computers, and *devices*, which include mobile equipment, wearables, and the growing world of the Internet of Things (IoT).[8]

Chapter Five builds and presents the results of a heuristic model examining the effect of circumstances (e.g., software quality, the proliferation of smart devices) and organizational choice on the overall costs associated with insecurity in cyberspace. These costs combine the losses associated with cyberattacks and the costs associated with implementing responses, such as the level of training, the acquisition of cybersecurity tools, restrictions on the connection of smart devices to the organization's network, and selective air-gapping of sensitive subnetworks. The model assumes a constant pressure from cyberattacks that first seek to suborn one or more of an organization's outward-facing computers (or smart devices) and then use that foothold to subvert the organization's network as a whole. The defenses consist of measures to reduce the ability to gain a foothold (e.g., better software, more training, limits on smart devices); measures to reduce the ability to convert

---

[7] *Browser sandboxing* refers to a tightly controlled environment that restricts permissions on what can be run (to prevent malicious code from executing or accessing something it should not, for example). *ASLR* is a process whereby portions of program code get placed at random locations in a computer system's memory every time the code is run. This way, attackers going to the same location to take advantage of a code vulnerability have a hard time because the portion of code keeps changing.

[8] *Internet of Things* refers to a near future when every electronic or even electrical device (e.g., a microwave oven) is connected to the Internet.

the foothold into a systemic compromise (e.g., cybersecurity tools); and measures to reduce the exposure of organizational assets to hacking (e.g., selective air-gapping).

Chapter Six offers summary lessons for organizations and public policy. While the optimal cybersecurity program is one that minimizes the total cost of cyberinsecurity (expressed as the sum of the resources spent on cybersecurity and the costs incurred because organizations are less than fully secure), no one really knows what that point is or how to get to it. And best practice is not necessarily optimal practice.

CHAPTER TWO

Chief Information Security Officers Surveyed

As a way to help ground our thinking in the current realities of the struggle in cyberspace, we talked to 18 CISOs.[1] We sought to gain their perspective on how they viewed the struggle today and how the struggle might evolve over the next two to five years. Our sample of CISOs is random in the sense that it was not systematic, but not random in the statistical sense. We drew on informal networks and opportunities that either presented themselves to us or were presented by our sponsor. Of the 18 respondents, eight were from services, four from communications, one from government, three from finance, and two from manufacturing.

We deliberately chose to emphasize depth over breadth in conducting the survey. First, we wanted to understand not only what CISOs thought about the struggle in cyberspace but why they thought as they did. Understanding the nature of the struggle in cyberspace required some background on how they got to where they were. Second, because CISOs worry constantly about security, they are not particularly apt to respond to external inquiries from people they do not know personally. Valid statistics could not be drawn from a feasible sample because of a combination of low response rates, the lack of true randomness in the sample, and the heterogeneous response base (for instance, how should the response of General Motors' CISO be weighed against the equivalent person working for a car dealer, the intelligence community, or the nonprofit sector?). Therefore, we mined our answers not to gener-

---

[1] We generally sought security IT decisionmakers for companies generating more than $100 million in revenue and employing more than 1,000 workers.

ate model parameters, but to suggest what elements should go into our analysis, as well as our heuristic model (see Chapter Five).

A motivating element of our questionnaire was whether CISOs thought the tools available to them to protect their networks were adequate in the current or forthcoming representation. If these tools were not up to the job, we asked whether they were looking for something radically different, where "radical" was defined by the respondent. We failed to find much evidence that CISOs were ready to open their windows and proclaim, "I'm mad as hell and not going to take it anymore!"[2] But this hardly means that tomorrow's cyberdefense tools will all be descendants of today's. Few people knew they wanted an iPad before they saw one, and not many people can specify a tool they will fall in love with tomorrow that has not been invented today.

Our findings are divided into three parts:

- common knowledge confirmed
- reasonable suppositions validated
- surprises.

The full questionnaire is contained in Appendix A (due, in part, to time constraints, the percentage of questions answered by all respondents began to drop off after the 15th question). By way of caveat, our reporting the views of CISOs does not mean we agree with all of their observations; in this chapter, we largely let them speak for themselves.

Common Knowledge Confirmed

Security postures are highly specific to the company type, size, vertical, etc.—and often, there are not good solutions for smaller businesses. The smaller the company, the smaller the resources available to buy cybersecurity solutions; thus, the fewer the solutions bought. As one respondent observed, "There are not a lot [of solutions] that are

---

[2]   This line comes from the 1976 movie *Network*.

the right size and fit for a small business . . . without a big check, there aren't solutions. Overhead is too much."

The importance of intellectual property varied with the individual firms' missions. Some have intellectual property, such as source code, to protect; one respondent in the insurance business mentioned written risk calculations as sensitive intellectual property. Others are concerned about strategic company information, such as a new product being released or marketing plans. Given the distribution of our respondents by class of business, it is not surprising that many spend more energy on protecting their customers' intellectual property (even from each other) than protecting their own. In one case, it was observed that an industry did not put enough emphasis on securing manufacturing systems. Although there were multiple oblique references to state actors, China (the most likely state actor) was mentioned only twice: once with respect to pressure from Congress, and another time to illustrate how hackers could steal more intellectual property than they know what to do with.

Cybersecurity is a hard sell, especially to chief executives (unless they or someone they depend on has been breached). To quote one CISO, "No attacker is going to call up a company and tell them what a good job they are doing at keeping them out." CISOs rarely get requisite support from those in lower-tier C-suites (e.g., operations, marketing, finance, business support). Almost every chief executive officer (CEO) can be expected to pay attention to cybersecurity at some point or another (although two respondents indicated otherwise), but most pay attention only when forced to—when something happens to their organization, or (less frequently) when something happens on the outside that forces them to re-evaluate the risk to their organization. Several respondents indicated that their CEOs spent 5 to 10 percent of their time on cybersecurity. Other CEOs delegate the cybersecurity oversight role to a committee—suggesting equal discomfort with ignoring the issue and with handling it directly. The consensus was that CEOs will be forced over time to deal directly with cybersecurity and to become more confident that they can weigh in intelligently, but this transition will not happen overnight.

CISOs generally agreed that there was no way to know whether they were spending enough money, but respondents split between those who thought spending was sufficient and those who felt more was needed. Either way, they felt that spending was likely to rise substantially. One CISO was as inclined to double the cybersecurity budget as to halve it. Another observed that "enough" was not enough. A common metric cited by several CISOs was what percentage of the IT budget went toward cybersecurity. Some CISOs had a shopping list against which to judge adequacy; some judged spending as adequate if it was rising. One respondent argued that every investment made in security was justified with how long they could avoid downtime. Still others looked at spending levels relative to potential loss levels, or considered whether their spending pattern addressed symptoms or causes. One respondent said anyone who answers "yes" to the question of adequacy does not understand the threat.

Air-gapping is known to be a useful option, employed by almost all organizations surveyed, albeit with a mix of physical and/or virtual isolation.[3] As a rule, the decision to isolate machines is strongly related to what organizations think employees and even customers will put up with (Libicki et al., 2011). But organizations that have valuable intellectual property, especially directly related to the care of customers, were particularly aware of the usefulness of isolation. Malware testing was an obvious candidate for air-gapping.

Responding to the desire of employees to bring their own devices (BYOD) and connect them to the network creates growing dilemmas. Some organizations do not allow such devices at all. Others allow certain models or applications because provisions are in already place to safeguard integrity and confidentiality. One respondent mentioned BYOD as an opportunity rather than a problem because "consumerization is going to drive things" in this world, but still did not allow unimpeded access to the corporate network. A university represented among our interviewees was completely hands-off. Legal issues associated with commingling personal and corporate information were also noted. The most

---

[3] The efficacy of virtual air-gapping as compared with physical air-gapping remains to be determined.

common approach is to allow access if organizations support mobile device management suites, remote wipe/kill, or full-device encryption (e.g., specific services mentioned included Good Client, Active Directory, and Bitlocker). Tellingly, no correspondent cited a specific instance of a system being compromised through a user-owned device.

CISOs feel that attackers have the upper hand, and will continue to have it. Optimism was the exception. One CISO thought that things might be better in two years; another, in five years—and this was mostly because many organizations have just started on the learning curve for cybersecurity and can only improve. But pessimism was deeply rooted among the rest of our respondents. "It will get worse before it gets better, and I do not know if things will get better," one observed. Another spoke of attackers dreaming of wealth and defenders not aware of how much they needed defense, and one observed that attackers were too smart, patient, and greedy to overcome. Other respondents noted that attackers shared intelligence and that they were getting cleverer; that they are benefiting from a "modularization of capabilities" (a reference to cybercrime markets); and that although defenders would improve over time, attackers would always be further ahead.

Reasonable Suppositions Validated

Customers look to extant tools for solutions even though they do not necessarily know what they need. They are certain no magic wand exists, and doubt the possibility of creating something radically different that could not be derived from today's range of solutions. Thus, the prospect of satisfaction seems distant, with respondents stating they were not looking to be satisfied, or that "satisfaction" was not the right word. One respondent went so far as to say security vendors were not expected to innovate. Others stated that they were not looking for a silver bullet, or that while they were not totally satisfied, neither were they looking for something radically different.

So what are CISOs looking for? Many called for integrated solutions ("a single pane of glass") that could bring together the point solutions of multiple vendors and, in doing so, filter (attack) signals from noise. One CISO wished for an ability to manage such point solutions "easily from a policy perspective . . . an ingestion perspective, and a metaphor perspective . . . [with] the ability to apply certain rules to everything at once." A related request was for a way to understand complex infrastructures that included internal and external elements as an ecosystem. Another would have liked a virtualized environment to help reduce dependence on vulnerable personal computers (e.g., thin-client plus cloud). Several others focused on the insecurity of the least secure client, with mentions of anti-phishing, reliable identity verification, and individual risk profiles; conversely, one noted that even the best users cannot avoid being phished 100 percent of the time. One respondent would have been satisfied with a better password management system; another wanted a sophisticated digital rights management architecture for data. Two cited deep factors, such as the capability (and desire) to build security into software and systems rather than add it on later, and the ability of an organization to understand the risks it faces. Another bemoaned the lack of good solutions for distributed denial of service (DDoS) attacks.

When asked what they would do if provided more money for cybersecurity, a majority of CISOs cited solutions that are human-centric, a broad category that encompasses training users to be more aware, increasing cybersecurity staffing (particularly to analyze the coming deluge of big data), auditing networks for preventable faults, and carrying out behavioral-focused analysis of attacks and attackers. The following arguments were made:

- Although tools are cheap and plentiful, it takes smart practitioners—humans in the loop—to get the fundamentals right. The need for greater performance favors products that generate an enterprise solution for sandboxing, white-listing, and the monitoring of networking devices.
- Cybersecurity governance is needed, especially audits that would both detect problems and alert management of where extra money might be needed.
- Lockheed Martin's cyber kill chain methodology (Lockheed Martin, 2014) provides a useful way of looking for soft spots in an

organization's systems, but employees must first be made aware of those cybersecurity threats.

- Security information and event management platforms, which aggregate logs and alerts into one dashboard for analysts, are also useful.
- International Civil Aviation Organization rules prevent people without passports from boarding planes: Why not have something similar for the Internet?
- Staff education and user awareness training are important in that the primary threat to the organization is from insiders—both those who were sloppy and those who did so deliberately. Such education helps reduce the impact of phishing and makes each user alert to the possibility of a cybersecurity breach caused not only by the user's actions but by the actions of others.
- Although a standard security architecture would take care of script kiddies,[4] it would not fare as well against organized crime, and would fare poorly against sophisticated hackers, particularly state-funded ones—especially when those hackers manage to make themselves look less sophisticated and get lost in the noise.
- With more cybersecurity employees, organizations can be more proactive in identifying potential incidents by putting people to work on log and event tracking, as well as on developing strategy and architecture for future systems.
- Well-employed people get more useful over time (even as hardware value decreases), and good people are needed to take on the advanced persistent threat (APT) and integrate their threat behavior observations with what others are seeing. Yesterday's need for analysts is today's need for scientists.
- Training employees more effectively to resist social engineering (phishing) must include tests to determine who needs more retraining.
- Understanding the top ten risks to an organization helps clarify what is important and prioritize investments.

---

[4] *Script kiddie* is slang for a hacker whose expertise is limited to following a script that someone else wrote.

But not every sought-after solution was framed in terms of people. Another common solution revolved around behavioral-focused analysis:

- Monitoring systems that detect anomalous behavior need to work in real time rather than by accessing after-the-fact system logs.
- Emulating specific threats reliably would be useful even though most threats enter via spear-phishing.[5]
- Systems could learn to make inferences about a threat's behavior in a network by examining the network's behavior (although a baseline would, unfortunately, shift radically with BYOD practices).
- A mechanism that permits security settings on systems to be adjusted and readjusted without human intervention would be useful, particularly when government specifications change.
- Tools should be available to protect data even if bad guys are in the network. (The respondent who mentioned this viewed current tools as point solutions unsuited to the range of extant threats, much less unanticipated ones.)
- Identity management is important but is essentially a subset of being able to inventory all devices and software, both authorized and unauthorized—to know who is touching the network. Therefore, role-based access is an important component of managing data from cradle to grave.

CISOs wanted information on the motives (intent) and methods (capabilities) of specific attackers, but there was no consensus on how such information could be used. Some respondents replied as if the purpose of understanding attackers was to prosecute them (e.g., it was consigned to the part of the organization that dealt with law enforcement). Others saw it as part of a broader intrusion defense strategy. One said this information is really "critical in the moment of attack." Another likened it to a "black art." Some organizations said they lacked interest in the matter or spent so little time and received so little value from collecting intelligence on attackers that they ignored the issue;

---

[5] *Spear-phishing* is a form of social engineering in which someone gets a phony communication that looks as if it was from someone they know.

another pointedly refrained from going "deep into the weeds to chase them down." Others were specific about the benefits of understanding who might be lying in wait for months or years until a specific weakness became apparent, or they remarked on the usefulness of understanding specific groups that might want to disrupt a major event (such as the Olympics). One respondent expressed awareness that although the organization lacked an army of people tracking all attackers, there were particular groups that the organization did need to understand. Those in the retail industry felt that they did, in fact, know who was coming after them.

Current cyberinsurance offerings are often seen as more hassle than gain, useful in only specific scenarios, and providing little return. Only a third of the respondents had insurance, but at least two of them noted that the insurance does not begin to pay out until high deductibles have been met (one respondent was, in fact, paid after an incident). Premiums are perceived to be high and coverage payouts limited. Strikingly, in no case was insurance central to the process of improving cybersecurity (in contradiction to how fire insurance practices promote fire safety); it was a matter handled by corporate finance people with, at best, some input from the cybersecurity department. There was little evidence that any cybersecurity standards were being imposed by insurers (perhaps because they dealt with the financial side of the house rather than the operational side), nor was there much indication that such standards made a difference in how corporations secured themselves. One remarked that the ISO 27000 standard and PCIDSS payment-card standard provided sufficient guidance. Another respondent noted that insurers were satisfied if the organization could brief a coherent cybersecurity story, regardless of the story's specific content.

The concept of *active defense* has multiple meanings, no standard definition, and evokes little enthusiasm. Definitions of this term stretched from legitimate and potentially useful scanning of one's own network looking for nonobvious indicators of malicious activity to legally problematic attacks on servers and networks used by hackers. Not one respondent admitted to the latter, although a few wistfully found the idea satisfying; one remarked that no one ever won any sports games by playing defense.

CISOs lack a clear vision on incentives. Many talked in terms of making their own management more aware of the cost of cyber-insecurity. No one wanted more regulations or added penalties. One shifted the question by arguing that vendors providing security software lacked the right incentives to produce quality products. Another observed that while security professionals had the right incentives, their corporate managers might not.

Information-sharing tended to live within a web of trust—specifically, peers in the same business space. Some aspects of sharing information with the government were deemed helpful, but there was still concern over how much companies receive in exchange for what they're giving ("a one-way street and completely useless"). Almost all organizations participated in formal (and, in some cases, informal) information exchanges with some part of the U.S. government; even foreign corporations did when they had a U.S. link. Opinion on the value of these exchanges was positive overall but depended on the parties involved. Among those earning positive marks were the defense industrial base pilot project, the Federal Bureau of Investigation (although regret was expressed that the agency is interested only when losses exceed $40,000), specific unnamed individuals within the government, the Cyber Information Sharing Partnership, and the Financial Services Information Sharing and Analysis Center.

CISOs tend to be optimistic about the cloud, but, apart from those who sell cloud services, most are willing to be only cautious fast followers; likely to wait until it is proven safe rather than live on the bleeding edge. The typical respondent noted the dilemma between new opportunities and indeterminable new security risks. Three respondents were very hesitant about using the cloud for storage or services because they did not believe they would track data in the cloud, control data in the cloud, or determine what data ownership even meant in the cloud. Several approached the cloud gingerly, starting from well-understood services (e.g., Salesforce, email) and then perhaps putting more-critical data there. One is thinking of using the cloud for "bursty" use cases. Another offers it to customers at the risk of complicating the organization's own cybersecurity strategy.

CISOs were more likely to assign a lower priority to security-as-a-service offerings, reserving it for specialties, such as network monitoring or analytics. (One, by contrast, was so committed to outsourcing as to boast of not knowing where the organization's firewalls were.) Because we generally spoke with representatives of large organizations and some had enough in-house talent to provide services to others, they would not be expected to outsource overall security ("we will deliver capabilities ourselves"). Someone mentioned *good* security as a service when asked for the closest equivalent of a magic wand.

CISOs, in general, are not ready to concentrate their purchases from a single vendor (but are not sure that heterogeneity is the best solution, either). Those who came closest expressed a willingness to contemplate other suppliers as a way of keeping their primary vendor honest. Some recognized that buying from multiple vendors reduced the odds of a catastrophic failure and assisted with pricing power. Others tried to straddle the question by purchasing security services homogenously but supporting a best-of-breed (an expression used by several) philosophy with respect to hardware. One CISO reminded us that most hardware was purchased elsewhere in the company.

Surprises

The effect of a cyberattack on reputation worried CISOs most, rather than more-direct costs. *What* actual intellectual property or data might be affected did not matter as much as the fact that *any* intellectual property or data were at risk. Two-thirds of all respondents specifically mentioned loss of reputation as the greatest possible fallout from cyberattack. A successful attack could undo the vast amounts of advertisement and effort put into creating and preserving a company's image. Those who worried most about reputation were afraid of cyberattacks that compromised confidentiality of customer data—an increasing concern given that personal information is becoming the raw material that corporations refine into sales. One respondent who manages data for others noted that the organization's key defense is ensuring that breaches into one customer's data do not spread to another customer's data; hence the need for a silo-based architecture. Several reported that attacks on them are really attacks on their clients (those who run clouds for their clients have to defend not just their own assets but those of others as well). Another respondent pointed out that the importance of the information lost to attackers was secondary; it mattered a great deal when *any* information was lost, however important or unimportant. It was understood that the reputation of an attacked organization is related to what customers know (or think they know based on what is reported in the media or news releases) about what happened, how they regard the organization's vulnerability vis-à-vis expectations, and how the organization's reputation stacks up against its competitors. Whenever something that could have happened to one organization happens to another, the CEO is quick to ask: Could it happen to us? Getting (and staying) ahead of regulators also came up: In essence, this is also an issue of reputation but before a different audience.[6]

In general, loss estimation processes are not particularly comprehensive. Two had a formal but undocumented process. Two had loss estimation processes limited to understanding the cost of post-incident remediation. Four had loss estimation processes that enumerated the types of costs incurred but did not try to put a dollar figure on them. Six had loss estimation processes without stated qualification. Four had no formal loss estimation process. The absence of an even halfway-satisfactory way of measuring the costs to reputation or the impact of loss of intellectual property might result from the fact that CISOs, vendors, and the security community as a whole focus on threats, rather than risks. Yet it is risk, not threat, that needs attention.

The ability to understand and articulate an organization's risk arising from network penetrations in a standard and consistent matter does not exist, and will not for a long time. Our respondents were all over the board in what they thought they needed (likely because every business is different), what tools to use, where to put their resources, how to use the cloud, etc. One noted that the most damaging threats were

---

[6] Worries from the telecommunications industry over DDoS attacks were restrained. From their perspective, it was not something they could not handle; they had more than enough capacity to do so.

those that were not anticipated: Although the organization was diligent in examining thousands of possible scenarios, its CISO still admitted to being "constantly surprised" by scenarios surrounding actual attacks. A second echoed this idea: The unknown threat is the greatest threat. A third noted that threats were broad-ranging, from script-kiddies to activists, criminals, and hostile states. The Edward Snowden affair also focused some CISOs on the insider threat; one respondent mulled that someone like Snowden could easily have been a co-worker. Risk calculations are often colored by recent events. One worried about a repeat of the DDoS attacks on e-banking in September and December 2012 (Perlroth and Hardy, 2013), and one worried about a DDoS attack in telecommunications, where they can be common. Another declared that the worst threat would be malware that converted computers into bricks, alluding to attacks on Saudi Aramco in late 2012 ("Aramco Says Cyberattack Was Aimed at Production," 2012) and on South Korean banks in early 2013 (Sang-Hun, 2013).

Some Conclusions

In an environment as increasingly complex and dynamic as today's large wired organizations have become, there is simply no well-understood paradigm for CISOs to use in minimizing losses to cyberattack. There is no "one-size-fits-all" solution in terms of tools, resource allocation prioritization, or policies. While CISOs generally know they need a better security posture as attackers continue to outpace defenders, there is little consensus and less clarity about *how* to go about increasing that posture. What little convergence exists is quite specific, however. There is a need for broad data analysis to detect the signal of attack in the noise of business. Better configuration management is also needed: knowing not only what was on the system but the software and connectivity state of every single box. Beyond this, basic truths still apply: Tool solutions vary, humans in the loop are still a large factor in the security equation, and perception matters a great deal—sometimes more than the actual substance of an attack. The best practice is not necessarily the optimal practice, and there is no silver bullet against hackers.

CHAPTER THREE

The Efficacy of Security Systems

This chapter reviews evolution of cybersecurity systems to the current state of affairs, in part to remind us of how the current system came into being, and in part to build a logical foundation for the parameters of the heuristic model presented in Chapter Five.

It was more than 25 years ago that the contest got under way between organizations wishing to defend information systems they had connected to the Internet, and the countermeasures used by those who wished to evade such defenses. Over time, the market and development cycle of tools, techniques, and defensive measures to mitigate both the likelihood and impact of attack steadily grew more sophisticated. Attackers have been quick to respond with their own tools, techniques, and countermeasures. Sometimes the same tools and techniques are used by both sides. Even with increased sophistication and technology innovation, it is not clear which solutions are truly necessary and which are superfluous.

Security concerns on the Internet began with the introduction of the Morris worm in November 1988,[1] and since that time we have witnessed the steady accretion of defensive capabilities within public and private organizations that now conduct much of their business using electronic networks (Avolio, 1999). In recent times, these capabilities have been referred to with such monikers as "defense in depth" and, as noted, kill chain management. But during the early and mid-1990s, there were not even de facto standards for systematic approaches to

---

[1] Networking preceded the Internet, and concerns about computer security date back to the 1960s. See, for instance, Ware (1967).

defense. Most organizations were in the early days of exploiting the Internet, and their understanding of its workings and associated vulnerabilities was rudimentary.

As one indication that networked information operations had not yet grown to their current importance, consider that only 10 percent of the 4,000 information technology departments surveyed in the mid-1990s had a chief information officer (Connolly, 2013). By the mid-2000s, the Internet had come into use for core business functions by most large organizations, and the need to understand the risks and potential costs of reliance on open system networks both inside and outside organizations had become critical to mission performance. By then, it was commonplace for organizations to have a chief information officer, and it quickly became standard to have a CISO as well—so that by 2011, 80 percent of businesses had a CISO or equivalent (PricewaterhouseCoopers, 2012). These changes reflected the scale and scope of the difficulty in protecting proprietary information while preserving the ability of employees and customers to interact. The risks of malicious hackers disrupting networks and stealing proprietary information had become significant; consequently, so did the costs of the personnel, systems, and services devoted to controlling those risks.

Measures and Countermeasures to Mitigate the Likelihood of an Attack

At the dawn of the Internet age, the defensive measures available to network administrators were fairly simple. They began with a firewall, a word so closely associated with electronic network defense systems now that it is easy to forget its more-physical origins. Early network firewalls were devices that concentrated Internet traffic into a manageable number of choke points at the network boundary of an organization, and then controlled or filtered that traffic by either allowing it to pass or rejecting it. These decisions were based on rules having to do with the type of application, the destination, and the channel or port on which communication was taking place. There were relatively few applications running across the Internet and through firewalls—such things as file transfer protocol (FTP), simple mail transfer protocol (SMTP), and network news transfer protocol (NNTP). These typically ran across standard channels or ports on firewalls (port 20/21 = FTP, port 25 = SMTP, port 119 = NNTP), and if the firewall were not configured properly, it was easy to slip things through on nontraditional ports or by using nonstandard protocol traffic on a port where the firewall was not looking for it. Since firewalls nominally have 65,535 ports, filter policy definition was easy to get wrong and susceptible to evasion by clever attackers.

Later, with the extraordinary growth in business use of the Internet, the number of applications rapidly expanded beyond this initial set, presenting many more modes through which attacks could be accomplished. As this transition has taken place, firewalls have progressively integrated previously separate capabilities that can naturally be invoked at Internet chokepoints—such things as authentication management and encryption. In many instances, CISOs purchase new capabilities based on new technical approaches created by venture-backed companies that are driven by attackers' countermeasures to existing defensive systems. One notable example of such a capability is the intrusion detection system (IDS), which still exists as a separate product category even as it has begun to be subsumed into the firewall.

Even before the introduction of the first commercial Internet browser in the mid-1990s, hackers were progressively refining their abilities to go undetected by the firewalls that existed at the time. For example, hiding the smallest possible malware payload in otherwise innocuous traffic necessitated that defenders examine traffic at a finer grain than the first generation of firewalls were designed to do (Roberts, 2012), thus giving rise to IDSs and intrusion prevention systems. Unlike city gate guards scanning whole people or firewalls filtering traffic by application type or communication channel, IDSs had to find purposeful flaws hidden in legitimate traffic. They use a technique known as signature matching and deep packet inspection, which involves quickly comparing packets of live network traffic against stored signatures of packets known to contain malware payload. These signatures are like a fingerprint; they uniquely identify suspicious traffic (malicious, like an exploit, or innocuous, like an attempt to gain unauthorized access).

As has been the case with firewalls, IDSs have been subject to a continuous measure-countermeasure process: As new exploits are discovered, new signature rules are written and applied and old ones are retired. There is a diverse and complicated supply chain for signatures for known attacks, some available publicly and others through paid subscription. This measure-countermeasure process has also witnessed the introduction of hacker innovations, such as malware polymorphism (exploit code that mutates while preserving function); payload parts and features, such as crypters, packers, and binders; and obfuscation methods that make known malware undetectable from antivirus systems and IDSs, as well as their associated defensive responses. Although IDSs are acknowledged to effectively detect evidence of incipient exploits for which signatures are known and readily available, new ("zero-day") exploits continue to appear, and it takes time for the defense information supply chain to provide defenders with countervailing signatures. The same is true for fixes that defenders must make to computer and network operations software that are common targets of attackers—it takes time to understand newly disclosed vulnerabilities in sufficient detail to engineer robust fixes, and even more time to implement those fixes.

Attackers and Defenders Often Employ the Same Tools and Techniques

One interesting feature of this exchange is that while defenders' interests are well served by rapid, extensive, public distribution of new signatures, a discerning attacker can use this information to suggest new vectors of attack. Another area where the measure-countermeasure competition has a symbiotic quality is network penetration testing. Defenders regularly engage in such testing, which involves purposefully attacking a computer system to find security weaknesses, to confirm the success of their efforts to make systems more attack-resistant. But hackers can use these same tools, and one open-source assemblage of pen-testing platforms known as Kali Linux (formerly known as BackTrack) has become one of the most widely used platforms by both malicious hackers and defenders (Dalziel, 2013).

Security Product Development Has Sped Up

Since 2000, there has been rapid growth in defensive systems that focus on examining network traffic, alerting on potential exploits or malware observed, and responding to prevent or limit damage from these exploits, either automatically or through human intervention. These now include not only the firewall and intrusion detection or prevention system but separate virus scanners, web content filters, data loss prevention (DLP) systems, virtual private networks, and the like. DLP systems are a representative example: These were introduced in the mid-2000s because the firewalls and IDSs of the time were not very "content aware," meaning they were not able to decode document payloads on networks in real time to prevent specific classes of content (identifiable by subject matter keyword, sensitivity marking, and the like) from leaving an organization's network. DLP systems introduced the possibility of enforcing restrictions on the movement of data and documents based on their specific content, adding another layer of protection to prevent exfiltration of proprietary or sensitive information. This category of security product did not exist before 2004, yet by 2013 the Gartner Magic Quadrant for Content-Aware Data Loss Prevention contained a dozen different vendors (Barney, 2013).[2]

The Shift from Signature-Only to Behavior-Based Detection

In recognition of the limitations of signature-based analysis of network traffic (including the time lag between initial attack and availability of

---

[2]   It is unclear whether DLP can remain effective against data that are encrypted, either by the nature of the communication or because the relevant malware has encrypted material to evade DLPs.

either a signature or a patch), defenders began to put more effort into behavioral anomaly detection. These approaches define normal patterns in network traffic or individual computer operations and then scan continuously for patterns that depart from the norm sufficiently to cause information system operators to suspect malicious activity. These approaches escape the limitation of being able to alert only on specific signature matches, and they have the potential to discover evidence of zero-day exploits through identifying unusual behaviors.[3]

Having More-Sophisticated Tools Do Not Necessarily Equate to Smaller Error Rates

Any process for detecting malware—whether based on signature matching, degree of deviation from normal behavior, or some other technique—is subject to errors of commission and omission, or false positives and false negatives. This significantly complicates the defender's task and presents opportunities for the attacker. Alerts based on signatures or behavior profiles are not certain; rather, they have an associated likelihood that they indicate malicious activity. It is thus commonplace for defensive systems to label traffic as good when it is in fact bad (for lack of having generated a signature match or anomaly indicator), or bad when it is fact good (for having erroneously generated a signature match or anomaly indicator, or when legitimate user behavior looks like intrusions and anomalies). This latter issue of false positives has been a profound problem since the early days of network security products, such as firewalls and IDSs. It is not easy to determine when legitimate user behavior looks like an intrusion or an anomaly. The generation of false positive alerts by cybersecurity products can easily overwhelm human operators' capacity for evaluation and action.[4] This

---

[3] For instance, Cylance has analyzed hundreds of malware signatures and detected previously unidentified malware that used zero-days.

[4] Several months after the Target penetration, it was revealed that Target had been warned by FireEye that something was amiss in Target's network. This warning was apparently ignored (see Riley et al., 2014). Not reported was how often Target had received similar warnings, which, upon investigation, proved to be false alarms.

problem is compounded by the fact that most information security managers buy a number of different products to address different avenues of potential exploit, and they must choose decision thresholds for each that result in a manageable total number of false positives.

Attackers prefer to hide by making their attack invisible. For example, they reduce the likelihood that evidence of their malware or exploit will be observed by hiding their needle in a haystack of network traffic.[5] This approach relies on the layered defense system lacking the fidelity to find the needle, or to observe the needle entering or transiting the network. Once the defender perfects a technique for finding a particular type of needle, the attacker devises new needles based on detailed knowledge of how the existing defenses operate. The attacker can also put more hay on the pile by introducing nuisance malware that is close to the defender's alerting and decision thresholds, introducing additional false positives and noise into the system. Well-financed attackers can maintain detailed knowledge of the latest approaches that defenders are using because most of the defensive systems, software, and signatures are widely commercial available. Plus, attackers can often test against freely available malware-detection systems (e.g., VirusTotal).

With each wave of innovation on the part of the defense, the problem of managing false positives recurs. Some of the more-recent innovations have been directed specifically at reducing false positives from previous generations of technology. This happened during the evolution of intrusion detection systems, when defenders recognized that having a high-fidelity map of network resources, such as server instances and software services, could allow the defender to selectively invoke protections, instead of needing to treat every system as vulnerable to every bit of malware. This desire to improve the marginal value of defensive responses is also an important motivation for the recent growth in threat intelligence services that use such methods as Internet service mapping to identify potential threats of high importance and to distinguish these from more-prosaic threats. They routinize the

---

[5] Alternatively, attackers might have launched DDOS attacks to create so much noise as to hide their entry into or presence within a system.

characterization of external actors, helping defenders anticipate specific sources and methods for new types of attacks.

Measures and Countermeasures Developed to Mitigate the Impact of an Attack

All these approaches have to do with defenders improving the fidelity with which they identify the presence of attacker code on their systems. But there are also a class of defensive approaches that assume attackers will get through no matter what is done to stop them, reasoning that it is fundamentally impossible to get an encyclopedic list of malware signatures. These approaches focus on mitigating the impact of attacks and rely on such methods as deceiving attackers about the identity of information resources or isolating the execution of attackers' computer code introduced in controlled circumstances.

One such approach involves defenders employing polymorphic techniques that have long been a staple for attackers wishing to hide from anti-virus software.[6] Defenders can now harden website software against traditional hacking methods by preserving the function of their web server code while regularly changing how it is expressed, so that it is unintelligible to the attacker (Shape Security, undated). Another approach uses "honey nets" that look and behave like the information resources the attacker is attempting to exploit but are actually bait that expose the attacker's actions to detailed observation while preventing RCX or a data breach. A third approach is the dynamic execution environment or sandbox, in which all programs carried within network traffic are allowed to run in a quarantined environment before being allowed to run in the end user's environment. This allows for controlled and isolated execution of malware without exposing the organization's employees and data directly. As with defensive techniques that attempt to identify attacker traffic as it enters the organization network, these obfuscation and quarantine approaches are themselves subject to coun-

---

[6]   One example is the company Shape Security, which uses polymorphism to make it harder for attackers to infiltrate and insert their malware.

termeasure once attackers become aware of how they work. For example, malware can detect being located in a sandbox, and wait to execute until on a viable target system; other payloads have a timer enabled that lasts longer than the defender's observation.

Defenders have also attempted to improve the security of their information and systems by changing the very nature of the computing and communication architecture in which they operate. In one approach, defenders physically isolate familiar software and computing instances from open system networks so that they are not accessible to attackers. These are commonly referred to as "air-gap" methods, and they separate the physical networks from the open Internet, making it more challenging to gain entry. This approach is commonly used in networks intended for national security applications, and selectively used in commerce for sensitive applications, such as telephonic switching control. It is relatively expensive because it requires dedicated physical infrastructure, but also relatively effective in keeping out unauthorized users.

A different architectural approach is to change the types of software or computing instances that are used. One such technique is called "moving target defense," in which open-system Internet resources are still used routinely by the defender, but software or server instances are replaced frequently, making it more difficult for attackers to establish malware that will persist long enough to exploit underlying vulnerabilities in the defender systems. While air-gapping and moving target defense are still uncommon, they are representative of hybrid approaches that defenders can use to resist attackers without giving up all the benefits and efficiencies of using Internet technologies for the foundation of their organization information systems.

Figure 3.1 provides a limited overview of some measures and corresponding countermeasures created and used by defenders and attackers.

Figure 3.1
Diagram Depicting the Measure-Countermeasure Dance Between Defender and Attacker

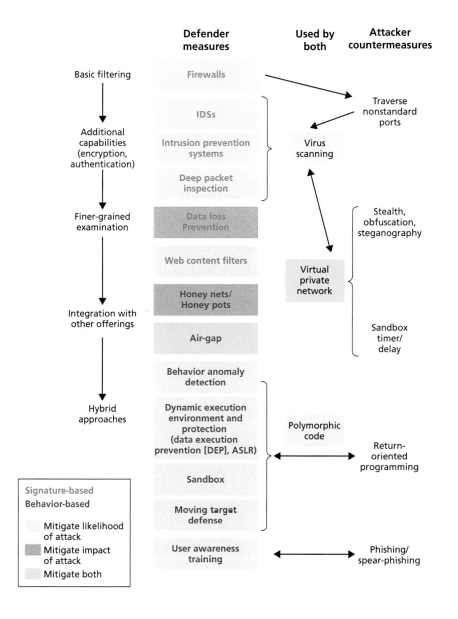

Human Element Continues to Be a Great Weakness

Whichever technological approaches the defender uses, it is always possible for the attacker to directly exploit behaviors of unwitting human users through "social engineering." Humans often are, and will continue to be, a weak point in an organization's defense. If an attacker can persuade a member of the defending organization to willingly part with access information, then the attacker can enter the network and compromise data and systems while appearing as a trusted insider. For an attacker participating on the defender network as a trusted insider, there is no need to worry about techniques for hiding in plain sight.

There are various methods of social engineering that give attackers as good or better access to network and information resources than if they had gained access through malicious hacking. One of the most persistent problems for defenders is the use by attackers of fraudulent but seemingly legitimate Internet communications (e.g., email), a practice referred to as phishing. It is difficult for every member of a defender's organization to be persistently and perfectly vigilant in identifying Internet communications directed at them by seemingly known sources, but whose contents (an Internet link, a file, a survey, a photograph, etc.) actually contain attacker malware. There is a healthy segment of the software tools and training market devoted exclusively to helping employers better prepare their employees to identify and avoid phishing communications. But without constant testing and red-teaming (hiring hackers to attack a system for the purpose of discovering weakness in its security), these solutions are often ineffective. Complacency is one reason; another is that new forms of communication appear regularly, and with them come new forms of phishing attacks. Ultimately, the problem might not be solvable. One cybersecurity expert noted that, if there were two of him, his bad self could probably find a way to spear-phish his good self.

A Cycle of Market Offerings

As the preceding paragraphs suggest, attackers and defenders are locked in an interminable innovation struggle. In the mid-1990s, there was a flurry of innovation in initial firewall functions, followed by a responsive flurry of malign hacking to circumvent them. This was followed by innovations in such areas as intrusion detection and prevention systems and DLP that have had long lives as independent product categories. As these functions matured, they began to be integrated into the firewalls themselves. But these functions rarely ever go away. Rather they accrete, and the defender is faced with continuously evaluating the net benefit of adopting the next wave of technology innovation. Initially, a new defensive innovation, such as the dynamic execution environment, is understood only by the most sophisticated and capable defenders, and even these organizations find it challenging to integrate these new approaches into their defensive strategy. Then a number of well-recognized large organizations adopt the innovation, and it becomes more acceptable to organizations with average defensive capabilities, often coming to be viewed as necessary. When innovations are first introduced, they are purchased and deployed by the most capable defenders as "best-of-breed" solutions, often because they are exclusive or have few providers. This provides incentive for other entrants to design and market similar solutions, and over time these become so ubiquitous in deployment that they are almost commodities.

Network IDSs are one example of this, having first appeared as a separate class of commercial product in the mid-1990s with such offerings as Wheelgroup's Netranger and Internet Security Systems' RealSecure. These companies were subsumed by Cisco and IBM, respectively, and another generation of companies appeared in the space; e.g., Sourcefire and TippingPoint, respectively acquired by Cisco and 3Com. This process of innovation by new market entrants, the growth in use of the innovation, and the innovation becoming integrated into larger equipment and service offerings, is one that has played out in multiple cybersecurity market segments for more than 20 years. There are dominant designs that emerge in segments, but these are not particularly stable, and they are replaced relatively rapidly in response to innovations by attackers. It is not a rigid, efficient production system specifically designed to produce a standardized product.

In addition to traditional classes of products, such as desktop computers and servers, we now routinely see new combinations of technology emerge, the cybersecurity implications of which are unclear, and which are sometimes shown to introduce a new class of vulnerabilities for attackers to exploit. Take, for example, the IoT, in which all manner of items from toasters to automobiles to insulin pumps are connected to the Internet. This has resulted in rapid growth in points of presence on a network. This is one of the principal motivations for the updated Internet Protocol Version 6. But while IPv6 might eventually prove to have better security features than its predecessor Internet Protocol Version 4 (IPv4), it will most likely prove to have vulnerabilities of its own. The introduction into organizations of employee-owned network-connected devices is another case in point. Organizations are often playing cybersecurity catch-up as they allow employees to gain the productivity benefits of using personal smartphones and tablets to interact with organization applications and data. There are a wide variety of approaches in organizations to BYOD policy and procedure, and many commercial product and service offerings are directed at helping defenders to manage the risks of such devices becoming another means through which attackers can operate.

Another example is the introduction of public cloud infrastructure as a service (e.g., Amazon Web Services, Google Compute, Microsoft Azure). It is possible to use these services to inexpensively deploy software applications external to organizations, and to define the networks for these applications in software. This has created a new set of challenges for defenders, because there are no ready methods to invoke traditional defense methods (e.g., firewall or IDS) on software-defined networks in the public cloud. That is to say, until the patterns of traffic associated with the use of cloud services are sufficiently understood, it can be difficult to look at traffic patterns and detect the ones that are characteristic of an attack. This has led to a burst of innovative activity to provide defenders the confidence that they can employ the same kinds of defensive functions for their cloud-based applications as they do for applications deployed on owned infrastructure. Without further progress in this area, the utilization of public cloud might be constrained to some extent. Both defender organizations and public cloud infrastructure providers are highly motivated to address questions of cybersecurity in this new medium—and of course, attackers will also be highly motivated to thwart these efforts.

The years have seen an alphabet soup of systems offering defensive functions. CISOs are having a harder time determining what is necessary and sufficient. They struggle to figure out which solutions emerge because they are the best or simply because their vendors have the best marketing and reach. Beyond what is useful to defend against malign hacking and social engineering, there are also choices to make about software environments for employee productivity and business systems that can have profound security implications. For example, not all document and knowledge management applications are equal in terms of the frequency and severity of the cybersecurity vulnerabilities they display, and an organization's consumption of third-party software can introduce vulnerabilities both internally and for customers and distributors. Mounting an effective defense thus involves not only purchasing and deploying systems to stem the tide of malicious hacking against systems known to be vulnerable but also reducing reliance on systems that routinely experience new vulnerabilities.

Ideal Solutions Can Depend on the Size of an Organization

Mounting an effective defense involves myriad activities that include identifying vulnerabilities, assessing risks and potential cost associated with exploitation of those vulnerabilities, choosing and deploying systems devoted to defense, training employees, and so forth. The labor and operating expense that an organization chooses to devote to defense will depend on a host of factors, such as the size of the business, the labor and cash resources available for defense, and the potential cost of attacks. There is wide variability in the level of capability of organizations to mount effective defense, and the fact that these differences exist is generally known and exploited by attackers (SurfWatch

Labs, 2014). For example, businesses involved in large-scale financial services are typically at a high level of attainment in defensive capability. The transactions they support are of high value, and they often have multiple direct ties to trusted third parties, such as payment-card issuers and other banking institutions. The most sophisticated attackers tend to target these organizations because the potential rewards are large. Conversely, the potential cost of successful attacks is so large that financial service providers devote significant resources to maintaining effective defenses.[7] As these organizations have comparatively large budgets devoted to cyberdefense, they have the resources to hire professional defensive staffs at the highest skill levels and capability. Still, banks write off a considerable sum of money every year because of fraud and hacking. The problem is difficult even for those spending hundreds of millions of dollars per year on cybersecurity.

At the other end of the spectrum are small and medium-sized organizations that generally cannot match this defensive sophistication or capability. This is a matter of having not only the appropriate resources (in terms of manpower, time, or money) but also the mind-set—as the focus for smaller organizations is often on functionality and survivability. They might not buy all available defensive technologies or might not have staff sufficient to maintain and analyze available threat and vulnerability information, but the potential value of loss in reputation or of intellectual property might not be so great as for a large organization. It is not unusual, therefore, to see a major brokerage firm employ the latest defensive approaches, such as next-generation firewalls and dynamic execution environments, and to see a small consumer retailer choose instead to rely on older firewall technology and forgo the dynamic execution environment. If the most sophisticated attackers were to focus on smaller organizations at lower levels of defensive capability, they might improve their average likelihood of successful attack—but their total returns might well be smaller.

---

[7] In April 2014, JPMorgan's CEO announced that annual spending on cybersecurity would reach $250 million, up 20 percent from the year before, while staffing would rise from 600 to 1,000 people (Henry, 2014).

Even for the most sophisticated of defenders, the challenge of becoming proficient with many different technological approaches has become almost unmanageable. Many defenders choose to outsource some important defensive functions to specialists who can provide a particular service to a wider range of customers. For example, many large organizations do not conduct their own network penetration testing because the discipline is so specialized that it is difficult to hire and maintain native staff capabilities at the highest levels of capability. Instead, they retain a managed service provider who performs these functions periodically or as needed. Another specialized service that it is common for organizations to outsource is training against and monitoring for phishing attacks.

The availability of managed security services has grown rapidly in the past several years. It is increasingly common to see small and medium-sized organizations buy "security operations center" services from third parties, effectively outsourcing most of the process of providing defensive capabilities. This dramatically reduces the burden of recruiting and retaining professionals with sufficient skill and experience to build and maintain the defensive capabilities themselves.

As organizations grow, they typically go through an evolution in the way they approach cyberdefense. They might start off buying a firewall and intrusion prevention capabilities and refer to outsiders only to help assess the consequences of an attack or to periodically evaluate the suitability of their defensive strategy. As they grow, and particularly if they become of interest to more and more sophisticated attackers, they might install digital leakage prevention systems, end-point behavior anomaly detection systems, and dynamic execution environments. Further evolution might see them consuming cyberthreat intelligence services and taking a more-active role in trying to understand who is attacking them and why. The managers responsible for making both strategic and incremental or tactical decisions will go through a repeated process of evaluating need against available resources. In the long term, most large organizations end up both owning defensive systems from multiple vendors and cultivating long-term relationships with managed security service vendors of one type or another. Different defending organizations will choose different allocations of resources based on formal risk assessment (if performed), loss experience, staff capabilities, available budget, and other factors.

Some Conclusions

One of the hardest questions for defensive managers to address is: Where does it end? The differentiation and accumulation of defensive functions in multiple products and services has now been going on for more than 20 years. Yet the level of sophistication and capability among attackers continues to increase, and the degree of vulnerability of an organization's networks and information resources either increases or, at best, does not get worse. Rapid innovation takes place on both sides of the measure-countermeasure divide.

As a backdrop for defenders and attackers, we see new information service platforms being introduced (e.g., smartphones, tablets, mobile operating systems, elastic cloud computing, IoT) and new information services that change patterns of participation and behavior (e.g. social networks, real-time search). Attackers exploit vulnerabilities in new platforms and services, and defenders respond in kind. In a more-static innovation environment, it might well be that defenders could make steady progress in reducing exploits through some combination of defensive techniques. But it is probably unrealistic to expect a decline in computing platform and service innovation. On the other side, innovation on the part of attackers keeps pace in all phases of their operations.

If a larger proportion of Internet communications and exchange of value took place through means that were more hardened to attack as a matter of design, it might be possible for defenders to make systematic progress toward a more predictable competition with attackers. "Walled garden" software systems (where the provider controls all aspects of content and transactions) have generally proven to be harder to attack (and, conversely, easier to defend) than open systems. But there seems no reason to believe that closed platforms will increase in importance for the foreseeable future. In fact, the trend over the past 20 years has been in the other direction: greater reliance on open systems for both software and networking. We have yet to witness the innovations that will allow for long-lived, persistent, open systems that are dramatically harder to attack than current systems. It is difficult to say whether this is inevitable or whether we simply have not yet received the necessary inspiration.

CHAPTER FOUR

Improving Software

Software vulnerabilities are what allow hackers to induce systems to behave in ways that their designers never intended and their users hardly expect. Even though software vendors might aspire to having secure software (assuming it does not prevent getting their product to market), vulnerabilities have not yet disappeared and will likely continue to characterize new software products. Their persistence and recurrence arises from the increasing complexity of software (NRC, 2009; Anderson and Hundley, 1998) coupled with the growing awareness of the money to be made by exploiting systems. This is exacerbated by the proliferation of devices connected and made available in the IoT. Progress in reducing the frequency and seriousness of vulnerabilities would contribute to making cyberspace safer. Conversely, the proliferation of software without corresponding attention to reducing vulnerabilities could enable the emergence of new and more-troubling cyberattacks.

This chapter examines the process by which vulnerabilities are detected and eradicated as a way of developing a sense of both the forces that affect cybersecurity and the near and medium-term prospects for cybersecurity.[1]

---

[1]   Detecting vulnerabilities is a deliberative process. The process by which vulnerabilities are created is not (usually) deliberative, but a byproduct of coding techniques, and not covered in this chapter.

When Vulnerabilities Matter

All software inevitably and inherently has flaws, or bugs. Typically, there are anywhere from three to 20 bugs per 1,000 lines of code prior to testing, and one or two orders of magnitude less afterward.[2] Among bugs, *vulnerabilities* are those that create a security weakness in the design, implementation, or operation of a system or application (NRC, 1999). They can be binned into those that affect operating systems, browsers, and applications (Microsoft, 2013), and they can be the result of design (architectural) faults or implementation (coding) faults. Most are introduced inadvertently, but some are intentional (NRC, 2009).[3] An *exploit* "is malicious code that takes advantage of software vulnerabilities to infect, disrupt, or take control of a computer without the user's consent and typically without their knowledge" (Microsoft, 2013).

Just as only some bugs are vulnerabilities, not every vulnerability can be usefully exploited (eEye, 2011) because there is no code path from vulnerability to exploit.[4] The depth of the exploit can also vary.

---

[2]   From *Code Complete: A Practical Handbook of Software Construction* (McConnell, 2004):

> Industry Average: "about 15–50 errors per 1,000 lines of delivered code." This is usually representative of code that has some level of structured programming behind it, but probably includes a mix of coding techniques.

> Microsoft Applications: "about 10–20 defects per 1,000 lines of code during in-house testing, and 0.5 defect per KLOC (1,000 lines of code) in released product . . ." McConnell attributes this to a combination of code-reading techniques and independent testing, discussed further in another chapter of his book.

> "Harlan Mills pioneered 'cleanroom development,' a technique that has been able to achieve rates as low as 3 defects per 1,000 lines of code during in-house testing and 0.1 defect per 1,000 lines of code in released product . . . A few projects—for example, the space-shuttle software—have achieved a level of 0 defects in 500,000 lines of code using a system of format development methods, peer reviews, and statistical testing."

[3]   Intentional flaws can, for example, provide a back door for manufacturers to access later on for debugging purposes. See, for instance, Blue (2012).

[4]   For instance, one might discover a buffer overflow, but no pathway allows exercising that buffer overflow. Or one might discover a path manipulation vulnerability, where an attacker can grab a file from a location he is not supposed to access (a common example is by inserting a "../" to go up a directory to which the attacker does not have access), but the presence

Some vulnerabilities might enable an attacker to uncover something about a system's memory that should have been hidden (e.g., how the OpenSSL Heartbleed flaw resulted in leaking memory contents). Others will allow an attacker to gain RCX; the compromised system runs the attacker's code without the user's knowledge, much less consent (Microsoft, 2013). Whoever can execute some code on a system can usually run any code on the system (with a privilege escalation vulnerability, if necessary).[5]

Several methods are used to find vulnerabilities. The most straightforward method is through *fuzzing*—introducing large amounts of invalid, unexpected, or random data to a system in an attempt to make it crash or behave unexpectedly. Bugs found by fuzzing are more likely than other sorts of bugs to be found by two or more people.[6] It also helps if a hacker can investigate a piece of software or code from an unusual angle (e.g., a section that is not documented), or can reverse-engineer the source code or associated binaries. The best vulnerability researchers have a sense of which bugs will not be found by others; whatever fuzzing they do is used only as a starting point or supplementary tool.

The ease with which a vulnerability can be found or exploited is not necessarily indicative of its value or severity. A high-severity vulnerability that can be exploited only under very specific and rare conditions might be less valuable, or require less immediate attention, than a lower-severity vulnerability that can be exploited easily (Microsoft, 2013).

Zero-day vulnerabilities (or *zero-days*) are those vulnerabilities for which no patch or fix has been publicly released; in some cases, the soft-

---

of a vulnerability (i.e., the attacker can move around in the file system) does not mean the implementation is available (perhaps there is a fixed/static file that is not part of any other directory, thus, nothing an attacker enters will ever get to that desired file location).

[5] Gaining RCX allows a hacker to run code only at the privilege level associated with the malware itself. However, there are privilege escalation exploits that can be used to gain root access once code execution is gained. There is no guarantee that this capability is known by the person running some code, or even if one exists (but for most operating systems, they do).

[6] The more-subtle vulnerabilities tend to require reverse-engineering the source code and gaining access to private symbols (information used to help debug code, typically containing function and variable names). For more details, see Microsoft (2014b).

ware vendor might not be aware of the vulnerability. A *zero-day exploit* works against zero-day vulnerabilities. Zero-day exploits are extremely valuable, as every system that runs the software has the vulnerability

Markets for Zero-Days

Vulnerability markets have been growing more popular in recent years; they can be segmented into white, gray, or black markets.

White-market buyers turn their purchases over to the vendor so that they can be fixed (and, in some cases, to provide signatures for IDS systems). *Gray-market* buyers tend to work for government or intelligence agencies (even if sometimes they return the vulnerability to the vendor); they prefer proofs of concept[7] (POCs), or something just shy of an exploit (pseudo-exploits) and some evidence that a vulnerability can be exploited for offensive purposes (e.g., to affect a particular target) or defensive purposes (e.g., to create customizable defensive signatures). *Black-market* buyers use vulnerabilities for crime; they prefer purchasing exploits, not just the associated vulnerabilities.

The gray market is thought to be more lucrative than the black market, and both are distinctly more lucrative than the white market.[8] Many estimates put prices in the gray and black markets at ten times those of the white market.[9] This is true, in part, because buyers in the gray and black markets are paying not only for the vulnerability but

---

[7] A POC demonstrates that a fully functional exploit is possible on a target system but it does not include final steps to make it weaponized (this is done by clients armed with specifications about a target environment and containing the necessary obfuscation or evasion capabilities). One test is the ability to cause the calculator program (calc.exe) to open up on a desktop (the "pop calc" test).

> The presence of a Chinese version of 'calc.exe,' the official calculator provided in Microsoft Windows, is interesting. Not only is it one more indicator of a probable Chinese origin, but also an indicator that this server was probably used as a test base, in addition to being operational and controlling infected machines from different targets (Bizeul et al., 2014).

[8] Based on interviews with gray- and white-market participants.

[9] Based on interviews with gray- and white-market participants.

for a guarantee that a vulnerability is exploitable.[10] As we will explain later, mitigation bypass techniques that enable classes of vulnerabilities tend to command much more money than single vulnerabilities can.[11]

The white market includes bug bounty programs run by software vendors, such as Facebook, Google, Microsoft, and Mozilla (Facebook, undated; Google, undated; Microsoft, 2014a; Mozilla, undated); independent bug bounty groups, such as BugCrowd and HackerOne's Internet Bug Bounty; contests, such as Pwn2Own;[12] and brokers, such as Verisign's iDefense and TippingPoint's Zero Day Initiative (BugCrowd, undated; HackerOne, undated; TippingPoint, undated; Verisign, 2014). Google's Project Zero, announced in July 2014, has hired some notable bug-hunters to look for vulnerabilities in Google's own and other vendors' software (Google, 2014). The white market tries to pull in security researchers by making their case on ethical grounds, citing responsibility to disclose, and offering recognition in lieu of high payouts.

The gray market drives up the prices that vulnerabilities can command, recruiting talent and participants based on financial incentives. It can use several business models. A client could subscribe to a vulnerability, exploit, pseudo-exploit, or POC feed. A gray market vendor could develop and deliver custom-made exploits, or sell a number of vouchers to a client and share information about various vulnerabilities, POCs, or pseudo-exploits available, acquired by cashing in the vouchers. This last model can often leave many vulnerabilities or exploits "on the shelf" to expire, because none match clients' needs. Gray (and black) market vendors can charge a fee for every month that a vulnerability remains unpatched and undetected from anti-virus and IDSs. Some gray-market vendors specialize: One might focus on

---

[10] Proving something is true (i.e., there is a viable way to exploit a vulnerability) can be difficult.

[11] Exceptional single vulnerabilities can command very high prices.

[12] Gray-market participants (including brokers) might agree to use only known techniques in contests, such as Pwn2Own, so as to keep new techniques a secret from white-market vendors. *Pwn* is hacker-speak for the ability to control a network/system; originally a corruption of *own*.

browsers and desktops, another on web-based applications and servers. Some vendors will work only with certain organizations, companies, or agencies. Other vendors are not particular about what types of vulnerabilities they try to find or who they sell to. Many believe that the U.S. government drives the gray-market economy, using defense contractors as middlemen and boutique shops in the lower tiers (Fung, 2013). The U.S. government and defense contractors could be more open about buying zero-day vulnerabilities,[13] particularly given concerns that the middlemen buyers might sell to others, ultimately transferring products into very dark places. Still, gray markets are legal, and even white-market participants argue that they remain so, lest activity that sometimes benefits vendors be pushed into black markets.

Black markets are organized by and run for cybercrime (Ablon, Libicki, and Golay, 2014). They deal in exploit kits, botnets, DDoS, and attack services (as well as the fruits of crime, such as stolen credit card numbers and bots). Only a very small portion of the black markets deal with zero-day vulnerabilities and exploits—which have little value for mass market malware, much less ordinary cybercrime. Black markets are more likely to deal in "half-days" (or "1-days" or "2-days"), vulnerabilities for which a patch is available but not yet widely implemented.

Few operations are capable of both finding and selling zero-day vulnerabilities; these likely number only in the low thousands. One market source proposed that roughly two-thirds of those who find one zero-day vulnerability do not find any more. As systems change and defenses get harder, previously prolific hunters can grow obsolete quickly. One expert suggested a three-year cycle of people and skills. Because of these waves of new participants, incentives must continually change. Participants flip between markets as their skills, ethics, and motivations (e.g., recognition, compensation, and intellectual challenge) evolve.

Recognition can come by releasing information about a vulnerability to the public (sometimes without first notifying the affected vendor), winning a contest (such as Pwn2Own), being recognized in a bulletin or advisory (which sometimes results in job offers), or getting

---

[13] For the U.S. government's part, this is already beginning to happen, starting with Vice Admiral Mike Rodgers, director of the National Security Agency (see Gallagher, 2014).

into a Bug Bounty Hall of Fame. Nevertheless, the ethics of disclosure are under debate.[14]

Compensation can flow to researchers when they are hired to do traditional penetration testing (attacking a computer system to reveal its vulnerabilities to its owner), sell to vulnerability brokers or other entities on any of the markets, collect bounties from vendors,[15] or with contest prizes.[16] Some researchers (and even brokers) save their vulnerabilities and cash in on the large contest prizes. Those who are in it just for the money will often bounce between markets chasing the payout.

As for intellectual challenge, Zero-Day Initiative (ZDI), a program for rewarding those who disclose vulnerabilities responsibly, claims that some of its best contributors prefer anonymity and thrive on the intellectual stimulus.

Table 4.1 provides an overview comparison of each of the markets for vulnerabilities.

The value of a vulnerability is largely determined by what it will do.[17] Higher values are commanded by those that allow RCX, affect a wide installation base, and work against desktops (rather than phones or devices). Different vulnerabilities will be valuable to different entities: Exploits that are good for establishing persistent presence are not nec-

---

[14] The two primary disclosure types are responsible disclosure and full disclosure. With responsible disclosure, all stakeholders (i.e., the vendor and the discoverer of the vulnerability) restrict information about a known vulnerability until a patch has been released. With full disclosure, the discoverer of the vulnerability discloses the vulnerability to the public first. In some cases, the discoverer will notify the vendor of the vulnerability, wait for a patch, and go public if the patch has not arrived expeditiously. Vendors have many priorities, and sometimes, researchers believe, need to be prodded by such threats. Ideally, a vendor would prioritize a patch based on risk to the user, but many vendors cast a keener eye toward public relations. Vendors, not surprisingly, believe that full disclosure should not be allowed, but there are no professional consequences for those who discover and disclose immediately—in fact, it can make someone more of a "rock star" in the community.

[15] Microsoft's Bug Bounty, which started in June 2013, offers a grand prize of $100,000 for bypass mitigation techniques (Microsoft, 2014a).

[16] Examples include Pwn2Own and Pwnium-4 (Hewlett-Packard Development Company, 2014; Chromium, 2014). Prizes can surpass $100,000 for successful exploitation.

[17] In general, once a vulnerability is shown to be exploitable through a POC (e.g., it pops the calculator), it is worth almost as much as exploits derived from it.

Table 4.1
Comparisons of White, Gray, and Black Markets for Vulnerabilities

	White Market	Gray Market	Black Market
Use of zero-days	Defensive only (used to make products or customers safer)	Offense or defense	Offense
Products	Vulnerability information only	Vulnerability information; PoC; pseudo-exploits; fully functional/ weaponized exploits	Vulnerability information; PoC
Participants	Bug bounty offers, contests, brokers.	Buyers are more interested in targeted type of attack	
Price	1x	10x	10x
Motivation to participate	Responsible disclosure (doing the "right" thing); notoriety; financial gain	Financial gain	Financial gain
Business model	Work directly with affected vendor; work through bug bounty; participate in contest; work with reseller (e.g., iDefense, ZDI)	Subscription-based; vouchers; or customized solution	"Half-days" are more prevalent

essarily good for conducting financial crimes. Vulnerabilities in critical infrastructure are believed valuable by infrastructure operators. A vulnerability can be worth less if the code base from which a vulnerability is found is subpar (i.e., if it has not gone through rigorous testing from a software development life cycle), is not well known or widely used, compromises the integrity only of a single user (e.g., cross-site scripting or structured query language injection), merely crashes an application (e.g., denial of service), achieves only an information disclosure or memory leak, or cannot be accessed or manipulated remotely.[18]

The ability to chain vulnerabilities to enable remote code execution adds further value. Exploits that can break a browser sandbox are quite valuable because they enable other vulnerabilities to achieve

---

[18] Local vulnerabilities can be used for privilege escalation, so they can be valuable—although they are not generally as valuable as remote vulnerabilities.

effects that go beyond, say, ruining browser sessions.[19] A memory leak vulnerability is made more valuable by its ability to bypass a defensive measure, such as ASLR.[20] It often is a chaining of three or four vulnerabilities together to achieve a desired effect, like breaking out of a sandbox or bypassing specific defensive measures.

In the Short Run, Vulnerability Discovery Might Worsen Matters

Ironically, a vendor's discovery of a vulnerability does not necessarily enhance cybersecurity immediately; it might initially make customers less secure.[21] Patches might be forgone,[22] delayed,[23] or just not work well. Some patches can cause new vulnerabilities (Okhravi and Nicol, 2008). Even if these fixes are implemented and an operating system is fully patched, there might still be other ways for malware or malicious payloads to access the system.[24]

Because malicious actors generally find out about zero-day vulnerabilities at the same time as the general public, they can take advan-

---

[19] Although *sandbox* has multiple definitions, it is used here to refer to code that isolates browser session faults to browser sessions rather than allowing malware to attach to the operating system.

[20] This is a technique to help protect against buffer overflow attacks. Portions of programs, such as stacks or heaps, are placed at random locations in memory when the program is first run, which causes the address of stack buffers, objects, etc., to be randomized between runs of the program. See Reece (2013).

[21] As of September 2014, researchers could conclude only that no one was affected by the OpenSSL Heartbleed vulnerability before a patch for the vulnerability was made available (Fisher, 2014)—but there were many victims afterward.

[22] Microsoft releases patches every month on "Patch Tuesday." This is when security patches and updates are released for users to implement. As such, "Exploit Wednesday" usually follows "Patch Tuesday," as users are not generally quick to immediately patch their systems.

[23] E.g., Oracle or Microsoft patch on a fixed schedule, but will make exceptions in special cases.

[24] This could happen through third-party applications running on the fully updated system. No operating system is immune to this. For an example on Microsoft OS, see Naraine (2012). For an example on OSX, see Fielder (2012).

tage of the consumers' slowness to patch. Even if some customers are dilatory, prudent ones often must first test whether patches break something elsewhere in their system; it does not help that disclosures and advisories that are released have less information in them than they used to. This complicates knowing whether a patch does what it should. Many patch advisories cite only "memory corruption," which is a catch-all for very different issues (e.g., "use after free" conditions,[25] buffer overflows[26]).

One study shows that after zero-days are disclosed, the number of malware variants exploiting them increases by 183 to 85,000 times, and the number of attacks increases by 2 to 100,000 times (Bilge and Dumitras, 2012). As Figure 4.1 illustrates, the window of exposure extends past the time between when the vulnerability is discovered and when a patch is released.[27]

Can Software Become Good Enough?

It is considered a sign of wisdom that people who run networks should always assume that their networks have been penetrated; accordingly, they should focus on determining the extent and nature of the penetration to better to limit the damage that such penetrations can cause. True, if a system has enough points that touch the outside world, the chances that at least one client machine (that touches the outside) can be subverted might be high, even as the odds that any other single client can be subverted is low; this reflects the laws of probability at work. If the odds that *any* one client is subverted can be driven low enough, at some point the odds that none of thousands of machines

---

[25] This is a condition where memory is referenced after it has been freed. Doing this can cause a program to crash, use unexpected values, or execute code (CWE, 2014).

[26] This is when data written to a buffer are bigger than the buffer allows, and the data spill over and rewrite parts of memory to which they should not have had access. This can cause erratic program behavior, a crash, or breach of system security.

[27] See also Frei (2013).

Figure 4.1
Attack Timeline

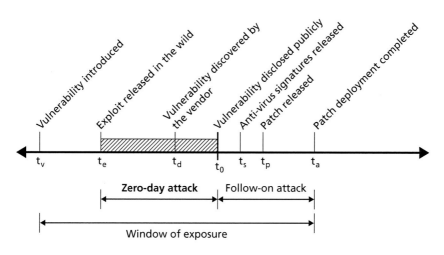

SOURCE: Bilge and Dumitras (2012).
RAND RR1024-4.1

has been infected can be raised to the point where many networks could be infection-free.

This raises the question: Is it plausible that someday software can be so secure that few, if any, hackers will be able to place malware into a system (without onsite presence or by exploiting human weakness), and even then only with great effort?[28]

The most optimistic software vulnerability model is that any one piece of software has a finite number of vulnerabilities and that once all such vulnerabilities are found and patches installed, hackers will have

---

[28] The human element, of course, must be taken into account, and organizations are always subject to some likelihood that a corrupted or rogue individual could create major damage—indeed, the more points that any individual can touch, the greater damage he or she can cause (as Private Manning and Edward Snowden demonstrated). However, multifactor authentication can overcome the human tendency to pick easy-to-guess passwords; good security engineering (e.g., restricted privileges) can prevent feckless individuals (e.g., those who blithely click on sketchy links) from allowing attackers to gain a foothold onto their systems; and systemic security systems can alert administrators to suspicious behavior by rogue or suborned employees.

no way in (human bungling aside).[29] Unfortunately, this model fails to account for the tendency of new software to replace old software well before all the vulnerabilities of the old software are discovered (as well as the possibility that new software introduces its own vulnerabilities). A Microsoft official observed that the succession of subsequent releases, coupled with the lead time associated with fixing vulnerabilities, meant that any one version would see only a limited number of patches before being superseded by its successor. Serious analysts believe that a more-realistic model of vulnerabilities reflects that their numbers are essentially unlimited,[30] but that the difficulty of finding successive vulnerabilities rises as the easier-to-find vulnerabilities are discovered and eradicated.

The popularity of products can also affect the rate of vulnerability introduction and discovery. For example, researchers increased their focus in 2012–2013 on web browsers (e.g., Internet Explorer, Mozilla, Chrome) and client-side products. As a result, more vulnerabilities were discovered and/or reported (TippingPoint, undated). Routers, cloud-based services, and server side vulnerabilities saw a decrease in the number of vulnerabilities found.

Do vulnerabilities deplete as they are found—either absolutely, or in the sense of increasing effort required to find the next one? In other words, are software vulnerabilities dense or sparse?[31] One seminal paper on the topic reported,

> We find strong statistical evidence of a decrease in the rate at which foundational vulnerabilities are being reported [for BSD Unix's core code]. However, this decrease is anything but brisk: Foundational vulnerabilities have a median lifetime of at least 2.6 years (Ozment and Schechter, 2006).

---

[29] The term *software* encompasses not only every application with sufficiently deep system privileges but intermediate software, such as browsers with built-in (but not necessarily flawless) sandboxes, and operating systems with their various built-in (but, again, not necessarily flawless) protections against allowing malware to take hold.

[30] See, for instance, Anderson (2002).

[31] Bruce Schneier brought up this debate in a May 2014 article (Schneier, 2014); Dan Geer revisited the issue in his keynote address at BlackHat 2014 (Geer, 2014).

The paper's data indicated that the rate at which vulnerabilities in the foundational code were discovered did, in fact, decline over time. Others have shown that there is weak support for the claim that detecting vulnerabilities depletes their pool (Rescorla, 2005). But *depletion* is a relative term. A perfectly bug-free piece of software is only an update away from having new vulnerabilities: Recent SSL vulnerabilities, Heartbleed and Apple's, occurred in newer versions dating from January 2012 and November 2013, respectively (Goodin, 2014a).

Another way of understanding vulnerability discovery and depletion is to look at the number of zero-day vulnerabilities that have been found more than once. A 2013 paper found that

> limited data from personal communication with a Firefox security engineer . . . indicated that there had been at least 4–7 vulnerabilities reported through the VRP [vulnerability reports programs] for which there had been two independent discoveries, a rate of 2.7 to 4.7 percent, which is consistent with what we see in our Chrome dataset (Finifter, Akhawe, and Wagner, 2013).

In another case, a four-way bug collision was reported to the organizer of Google's 2014 Pwn2Own competition (Greenberg, 2014). According to a 2013 paper, once discovered and disclosed, vulnerabilities are patched after an average of 120 days. Putting the two together suggests—as a rough order-of-magnitude estimate—that a vulnerability found by one person has a 10-percent likelihood of being found by someone else over the period of a year (if never patched). Put another way, if all vulnerabilities were of equal obscurity, the half-life for a vulnerability would be ten years before it would be independently rediscovered.[32]

One recently introduced metric of how difficult it is to find a vulnerability is the number of fuzzing test cases that have to be run to

---

[32] This assumes that the software base remains the same (major revisions can often eliminate a bug that no one knew was there) and that the vulnerability was not used as an exploit (whose discovery could then lead to the discovery and elimination of the vulnerability being exploited). This is also just one estimate. Other research finds that the half-life for vulnerabilities can be as high as ten months (Rescorla, 2005).

find a flaw. In a March 2014 Pwn2Own competition (Mimoso, 2014), Chaouki Bekrar, president of Vupen, observed, "The Firefox zero-day we used today, we found it through fuzzing, but it required 60 million test cases. That's a big number . . . that proves Firefox has done a great job fixing flaws; the same for Chrome." To some extent, the race between software companies and hackers (of whatever colored hat) to find vulnerabilities has a lot to do with how much fuzzing capacity each has (plus the efficiency of their fuzzers, which can vary greatly). In that regard, Google claims to have as many as 3,000 fuzzers running their code full-time; Microsoft has 200. To the extent that finding vulnerabilities in software takes an increasingly large number of fuzzing cycles, one could trace its increasing hardness over time and, correspondingly, predict the declining number of those capable of finding zero-days. As noted, though, fuzzing is not the only way to find vulnerabilities (and it does require gaining direct access to the software being tested inasmuch as fuzzing remote systems is far too noisy).

Given the difficulty of eradicating bugs in applications software, operating system vendors include mitigation techniques, such as ASLR and DEP, to thwart successful exploitation of vulnerabilities.[33] Microsoft now estimates that there are fewer than five mitigation bypass techniques per new installation of a Microsoft product. Return-oriented programming (ROP) is an example of a mitigation bypass technique. It can be used to bypass DEP, for example.[34] The low supply of mitigation techniques helps explain why the white market places more emphasis on paying for mitigation bypass techniques, and why they are worth more than just a vulnerability.[35]

---

[33] DEP is a security mitigation technique to prevent unwanted code from being executed. It is a technique where memory can be either writable or executable, but not both, which prevents an attacker from filling a buffer with code and executing it (Reece, 2013).

[34] Generally speaking, ROP is a way to leverage existing code (i.e., code re-use) to achieve some goal other than the code was originally intended for. ROP enables an attacker to control the stack to direct the next code execution to happen in a place of his/her choice. Often, there are fixed locations (even with ASLR, there still need to be fixed locations in code) that are executable (thus, DEP does not provide much prevention here).

[35] In fact, Microsoft has announced that it will pay $50,000 for defensive techniques against mitigation bypass techniques, as well as knowledge of attacks "in the wild" using mitigation bypass techniques.

The hope of effectively vulnerability-free software is buttressed by several data points. One is the iOS operating system, which has been much more successful at resisting malware than other mobile device operating systems, such as Android[36]—despite a user base that reflects almost a billion such devices having been sold as of July 2014. Granted, iOS devices lack necessary features (robust multitasking, easy customization) for widespread corporate use,[37] but they at least provide proof that malware-resistant devices are possible. Successive versions of Microsoft operating systems, which constitute most corporate and government foundations, are considered improvements over their predecessors. "Scans of real-world installations show that [Windows] XP systems get infected six times more often than computers running later editions, including Windows 8" (NV, 2014). A high-quality piece of code that goes through a rigorous software development life cycle, such as Microsoft's Security Development Lifecycle,[38] might have fewer easy-to-find vulnerabilities (e.g., bugs found through fuzzing), even if it still contains vulnerabilities that can be found through reverse-engineering or manual inspection. A decrease in active vulnerabilities can also result from faster patch release from vendors, and better defenses, such as the Enhanced Mitigation Experience Toolkit (EMET).[39] The aforementioned president of Vupen observed, "It's definitely getting harder to exploit browsers, especially on Windows 8.1 . . . exploitation is harder and finding zero-days in browsers is harder" (Mimoso, 2014). Indeed, "Left unscathed [at the 2014 Pwn2Own contest] was the highest single prize of the contest, $150,000 for the 'Exploit Unicorn.' This rare beast demanded a specific hack: system-level code execution on a Windows 8.1 x64, in IE 11 x64, with an Enhanced Mitigation Experience Toolkit (EMET) bypass" (Rosenblatt, 2014).

---

[36] This applies to devices that users have decided not to "jail-break."

[37] But see Cunningham (2014).

[38] See Microsoft (2014c).

[39] EMET is a free Microsoft tool to help users deploy and configure a variety of security mitigation technologies (including ASLR and DEP).

Figure 4.2
Both Offense and Defense Scramble to Be First to Find Flaws

RAND RR1024-4.2

Regardless, because of the emphasis of functionality over security, once a technology or device is released to the public, offense and defense sectors start searching for vulnerabilities—starting a measure-countermeasure game of offense (exploit) versus defense (secure). Sometimes the vulnerabilities are exploited first; sometimes defense catches the vulnerability first. Figure 4.2 gives an overview of the cycle of vulnerability discovery.

A Wave of (Connected) Gadgets

Many expect a growing number of devices and objects to be connected in ways that they have not been (and were perhaps never meant to be): for example, the IoT.[40] By the year 2020, the number of connected devices might outnumber the number of connected people by a ratio of 6:1 (Evans, 2011), and 26 billion devices are projected to be connected

---

[40] The title of this section provided with apologies to T. S. Ashton (1961).

to the Internet, up from 3 billion today (Gartner, 2013). Although the current primary thrust of the IoT is on the person or in the home, organizations might find themselves enmeshed in the IoT thanks to workers bringing their devices to work, as well as the increasing variety and reduced costs of autonomous sensors and controllers. All this would combine to form a greater attack surface.

Vulnerabilities from the IoT manifest themselves in two ways. Device protocols (in comparison with computer protocols) and software bases generally have not yet gone through rigorous vulnerability testing, either because they are proprietary or they are not well-known enough yet for security researchers to investigate them thoroughly.[41] Vendors might be only vaguely aware that their devices can compromise the networks they are connected to (and the systems connected to these networks), not just themselves. Merely adding Internet functionality to items that previously had no connectivity features, or that are not considered "traditional" Internet devices,[42] creates risks. Further, these devices often run older software that users do not think to patch or upgrade because the previous lack of connectivity obviated the need.[43] An additional consideration: Will consumers understand that a refrigerator with a 20-year lifetime also needs 20 years' worth of software patches?

The IoT poses problems for organizations in two ways. First, it can only increase the number of access points into an organization. An attacker unable to enter a network by pwning a personal computer might be able to obtain network privileges by subverting an unat-

---

[41] One example is the proprietary Z-Wave protocol designed for low-bandwidth data communications in embedded devices. In 2013, researchers discovered that the Z-Wave is susceptible to replay attacks (where an attacker can eavesdrop and record messages to play back later—for instance, a message to turn off a sensor) and poor implementation of cryptographic features (allowing an attacker to reset the electronic key needed to unlock a door). See Black Hat (2013).

[42] See, for example, how security researchers have hacked network-enabled lightbulbs to leak Wi-Fi passwords (Goodin, 2014b). Another example is adding Bluetooth functionality to insulin pumps.

[43] A few examples: 90 percent of ATMs run Windows XP; many satellite tracking packages run on Windows 95 or Windows XP.

tended printer or a smart thermostat. Second, and worse, devices are more likely than computers to be connected through wireless links. An organization might have assumed that it could inventory the devices on its system by polling all of its Internet addresses (or, more primitively, tracing its Ethernet cables). With wireless connections, any device sitting within radio-frequency range can potentially become part of the network—in some cases, by piggy-backing on a directly addressable device. Configuration management software might not be able to assess the security state of all connected devices if some of them do not register, or register in ways very different from computers and each other. Thus, the IoT might make it very difficult for organizations to know where their perimeter—or at least secure perimeter—sits. They might be subject to cyberattacks that gain access through devices that the organization did not fully realize was accessing its network.

That noted, the vulnerability of the things themselves is likely to differ from the vulnerability of computers. Computers are general-purpose devices; most things are not. Computer architectures are designed to allow the introduction of third-party instruction sets creating mechanisms that facilitate the acquisition of malware. IoT device architectures are less likely to require third-party instruction sets and should be more resistant to malware that requires modifying or "writing" new data to carry out a function,[44] though they might still be bricked in other ways. Conversely, computers have the processing power to do encryption and authentication, while the smaller things either cannot do so or are never asked to. They might be easier to hijack directly. While not true for all classes of attack techniques, some that work on computers also work on IoT devices (Gtvhacker, 2014). Examples of networks pwned because IoT devices have been subverted by hackers are few and far between to date—but how long will this remain true?

Although the IoT is likely to enlarge a typical organization's attack surface, a world without them is still a world in which the odds

---

[44] This does not prevent bad instructions from essentially turning the device into a paperweight—which might be a modest problem for an organization but not so modest if the device is, for example, a pacemaker.

of having systems penetrated remains too high, for several reasons. First, secure coding is not part of the standard curriculum for computer science majors. These students are the next generation of people developing and creating the devices. Second, a business's first priority is functionality, not security. Today's lean start-up culture creates incentives to introduce a minimum viable product quickly. Security is often an afterthought, which results in the sale of devices that are functional but riddled with security-related vulnerabilities. Third, introducing a vulnerable product and counting on being able to patch vulnerabilities as they are found is less expensive than creating a secure product; that is, one with secure coding supported by static analysis and vulnerability testing from the beginning.[45]

Some Conclusions

Two somewhat contradictory lessons can be cautiously drawn from this chapter.

The first is that there is the *possibility* that mitigation software can improve enough to put into question the assumption that attackers have to be defeated within the network (to minimize damage) rather than before they get into the network (to eliminate damage).

The second is that there is the *opposite* possibility. That is, the burgeoning set of network relationships arising both from the IoT and the many privileges that organizations conclude they must extend to other organizations makes the perimeter harder to identify and harder to guard. Thus, cybersecurity efforts must be based on the assumption that the bad guys are in the network (rather than fighting to keep them out), and security must be managed even more intensively at the systemic level, rather than by keeping attackers out of the system altogether.

---

[45] See, for example, Fisher (2013):

> For most companies it's going to be far cheaper and serve their customers a lot better if they don't do anything [about security bugs] until something happens. You're better off waiting for the market to pressure on you to do it.

CHAPTER FIVE

A Heuristic Cybersecurity Model

In this report, we have described the various factors affecting the choices that organizations can make about their cybersecurity and the possible consequences of such choices. This chapter draws on those factors to generate a heuristic model of cybersecurity.[1] Its aim is to illuminate these factors, put some plausible numbers behind them, and observe how they might interact. We seek to understand these forces systematically as a way of creating a *framework* for thinking about cybersecurity choices.

Although this exercise will yield forecasts, these forecasts should not be understood as predictions. On the one hand is the dynamic (measure-countermeasure) nature of cybersecurity, the need that the model has for simplification (to achieve tractability), the reliance on specific parameters to make the model work, and the assumption of well-informed rationality.[2] On the other hand, the data to populate and

---

[1] The purpose of a heuristic model is to increase understanding of important variables and not necessarily to make precise forecasts. We acknowledge that other models of cybersecurity exist, but they range in depth (i.e., static and diagram-deep versus programmable and dynamic) and emphasis (e.g., specific sectors). Most tend to focus on the defensive and/or reactionary point of view. A few examples include National Institute on Standards and Technology (2013); Hoffman (2012); and Cyber Security Strategies (undated). Reports with a supervisory control and data acquisition focus include Red Tiger Security (undated) and Brancik (2003). Other reports that examine global cybersecurity and impending risks include Cisco (undated); Mandiant (2013); McAfee (2012, 2013); Lancope and Ponemon Institute (2014); Hewlett-Packard and Ponemon Institute (2013); Verizon (2014); Ponemon Institute (2013b); and Industrial Control Systems Cyber Emergency Response Team (2013).

[2] An organization's decisions could be modeled as a search for the lowest cost, but, as Chapter Two described, CISOs typically have only a rough notion about the relationship between security measures taken and cyberattacks prevented. Furthermore, as members of

validate such a model simply do not exist—for example, who knows how much information is stolen that is never discovered? Together, these suggest that any predictions stemming from this model are notional. To paraphrase Richard Hamming, we seek insight, not numbers (Hamming, 1962, p. vii). To this end, our model has more than two dozen user-set (that is, rather than fixed) parameters, both to avoid excessive arbitrariness and to permit sensitivity analyses.

With that in mind, this chapter describes the structure of the heuristic model and discusses the more-salient results.

Model Structure

Our model portrays the struggle of organizations to minimize the cost arising from insecurity in cyberspace over an extended (e.g., ten-year) period. We do so knowing that ten years is a very long time in the fast-changing world of information systems, but we wanted to capture some long-term trends (e.g., the IoT) and the long-term effects of certain decisions, such as the choice of tools. The model's focus is on the evolution of cyberspace (notably the evolution of software and the proliferation of entry points, such as computers and other devices) coupled with the effect of decisions that organizations make to optimize their cybersecurity.

Organizations seek to minimize the total cost of cybersecurity, which we define as the sum of (1) losses resulting from cyberattack (which include intangibles, such as damage to reputation), (2) the cost of tools and training, and (3) the reduction in efficiency associated with limiting the benefits of connectivity.

To do so, organizations make decisions about the use of four different instruments:

- how much user training to offer
- how many cybersecurity tools to buy

---

large organizations, their choices and preferences might be shaped by institutional forces of the sort that make preserving the organization's reputation, rather than minimizing observable financial losses, its most important cybersecurity goal.

- how much to restrict smart devices (e.g., cell phones, smart thermostats)
- how much (if any) of the organization's network needs to be isolated.

Calculations are carried out in year 0 (e.g., 2015) and repeated in each year over a ten-year period. Changes over time include the number and vulnerability of computers and devices, the increase in the losses associated with cyberattacks, and the effect of countermeasures on the efficacy of cybersecurity tools.

We do *not* model decisions made by attackers. Attacks are portrayed as a completely exogenous force. Thus, the model does not consider such policies as law enforcement; intervention into black, gray, or white markets; or active defense (in the sense of levying costs on attackers).

Organizations

The model posits 1,024 heterogeneous organizations that collectively represent the entire world of cybersecurity (victimized individuals aside). These organizations differ in three attributes: *size, value* (at risk from cyberattack relative to size), and *diligence*. There are four categories of size, five categories of value, and five categories of diligence.

The four categories of *size* are organizations with

- a few hundred employees
- a few thousand employees
- tens of thousands of employees
- hundreds of thousands of employees.

The number of employees is a proxy for how many people have access to certain types of information or whose systems and users mutually trust each other. Size is presumed to have a strong influence on the likelihood that an organization's perimeter can be breached (smaller organizations have fewer entry points and therefore may be thought of as more secure, in that respect), as well as on the cost of training and tools (larger companies can more cost-effectively mount security training programs). The number of organizations in each of four size types is the same.[3]

There are five categories of *value* and five categories of *diligence*. The *value* categories measure the loss an organization suffers from a cyberattack. The *diligence* categories measure the ability of an organization to wrest value from the tools that it buys. An organization that evaluates the costs and benefits of various levels of cybersecurity protection would presumably take more steps if, everything else being equal, it is likely to suffer greater losses from cyberattacks (e.g., more value at risk) *and* if it can wrest more value from the tools it contemplates using (e.g., greater diligence).

Thus, there are 100 types of organizations (4 × 5 × 5), but the number of organizations within each three-attribute type might be different. The number of organizations within each of the four *size* classes is the same. But the population of organizations within any one *value* class and any one *diligence* class is distributed binomially: For instance, for every organization in the highest or lowest value class, there are four in the next-highest and next-lowest value classes and six in the middle value class. The same holds for the diligence-class distribution. They both use the 1–4–6–4–1 binomial distribution. To avoid having to talk about fractional organizations, our model assumes 1,024 organizations to be divided along three dimensions: size (4), value (16), and diligence (16).[4]

Under the press of cyberattacks, organizations must mount or at least contemplate some assortment of defenses to reduce the odds of being successfully attacked to less than 100 percent. If a successful attack could still take place, an organization might also take steps to reduce the loss from a cyberattack.

An organization's loss from a cyberattack is therefore a product of (1) the odds that an attack succeeds (likelihood of attack), and (2) the loss

---

[3] Although the calculations are based on 256 small, 256 medium-sized, 256 large, and 256 very large organizations, the size of organizations in the real world follows a power-law distribution. Thus, in our model, one large organization is a proxy for ten such organizations; one medium-sized organization is a proxy for 100 such organizations, and one small organization is a proxy for 1,000 of similar size.

[4]   4 × 16 × 16 = 1,024.

from a cyberattack's success (impact of attack). For purposes of simplification, we assume that an organization is successfully attacked no more than once per year and that the losses from being attacked in one year are completely determined by the year (the baseline loss rises every year in the model), the value class of the organization, and the share of the organization's value at risk accessible to the rest of the world (that is, that which is not air-gapped).

The odds that an attack can succeed are, in turn, a product of an organization's external hardness and internal hardness. External hardness might be understood as an organization's ability to keep attackers from establishing a beachhead within an organization's network. Internal hardness is the organization's ability to keep a beachhead from being converted into a successful cyberattack. In other words, hardness, both external and internal, can be considered as a probabilistic measure. When both external and internal hardness equal 0, then an attack is absolutely likely to penetrate an organization, and a penetration is absolutely likely to lead to compromise and hence loss of value at risk. If *either* external hardness *or* internal hardness is 1, then either an attack will be stopped at the border or no penetration will lead to a compromise.

An organization's external hardness, in this model, is determined by the number of computers it has, the ability of each to resist penetration, the number of devices (IoT and cell phones) connected to its network, the ability of each of *those* devices to resist penetration, the level of training its employees receive, and its policies regarding devices (e.g., its rules on BYOD). An organization's internal hardness is a function of the tools that it buys (e.g., intrusion detectors).[5]

Hence, losses=value at risk × (1–external hardness) × (1–internal hardness).

The models runs five subroutines in a specific order to determine an organization's losses from cyberattack. These subroutines represent parameters that were discussed by CISOs and are run in

---

[5]   In reality, some of these tools, such as firewalls or sandboxes, prevent penetrations. Fidelity, alas, sometimes has to be sacrificed in model-building in order to serve tractability and coherence.

sequence rather than in parallel to represent a progression from hope to painful commitment. That is, they hope that training users suffices; if that does not work well enough, they buy cybersecurity tools to thwart attackers; if the combination does not prove good enough, they work on restrictions, first to head off the burgeoning increases in addressable devices (IoT), and second to ensure that at least the most critical processes are protected through isolation (i.e., air-gapping). Each affects one of the three parameters: external hardness, internal hardness, and value at risk.

1. *Initial External Hardness:* First, the odds that every computer and device can repel an attacker are calculated based on the number of computers, the quality of their software, the number of devices, and the quality of *their* software. This determines an organization's initial external hardness. Note that this is the only one of the five subroutines not affected by an organization's security posture; it is completely exogenous.

2. *Training:* An organization can improve its external hardness by increasing the level of training (which can be understood to include, for example, restrictions on users' ability to make changes to their own machines and/or access organizational assets). The baseline assumes a minimal level of user cybersecurity awareness training.

3. *Tools:* An organization's internal hardness is then enhanced to the extent that it buys cybersecurity tools. In practice, organizations are forced to bring their operations up to prescribed cybersecurity levels (e.g., medical establishments are affected by the Health Insurance Portability and Accountability Act [Pub. L. 104-191, 1996]; stores are affected by payment-card industry standards). The model assumes such expenditures into a baseline; it counts tools acquired over and above that baseline.

4. *BYOD (and Smart Devices):* An organization can further increase its external hardness by successively reducing the number of connected devices it supports, in large part, by restricting what employees can bring into the network (and what business or

building-management devices are allowed to interact with the network).

5. *Air-Gapping:* An organization can reduce the loss from of a cyberattack by isolating parts of its networks where compromise might be particularly costly.

In the latter four subroutines, the organization evaluates increasing its effort until it reaches the point at which the costs of greater effort exceed the savings from reducing the costs associated with cyberattack. Appendix B describes each of these five subroutines in more detail.

Results

The heuristic model provides results and artifacts. Results reflect the interactions among the various forces that affect cybersecurity and their impact on the cost of securing cyberspace: the sum of the losses from cyberattacks, the resources required to mount such defenses, and the reduction in a network's value arising from the restrictions on its use. Artifacts result from how such forces are expressed in the equations and should be of no further interest (except perhaps as a warning to professional model builders). Unfortunately, they might interfere with interpreting the results correctly, and so merit a brief note.[6]

---

[6] Artifacts arise in large part because decisions to adopt policies are based on the incremental gains that such policies offer; they depend on the shape, as well as the size, of the curve that links effort to effect. For instance, an improvement in the efficacy of tools might or might not lead to their greater use. If such improvements mean that the first few tools are so cost-effective that they reduce the unsolved portion of the problem to very low levels, the organization might pass on buying more tools. Alternatively, if such improvements do not allow the first tools chosen to solve the problems, they might still raise the efficacy of later tools in ways that persuade organizations to buy more because they have become more cost-effective. Apparent nonlinearity is another artifact (particularly when using exponential functions). Consider the external hardness of an organization—a function of the base hardness (reflecting the number and vulnerability of computers and devices) and two policy instruments: training and BYOD rules. If the base hardness is sufficiently high, investing in training and limiting the access of devices to an organization's network buys too little additional security; they are just not needed. If the base hardness is at a medium level, such investments could make a big difference. If base hardness is too low, then such investments, again, buy

We start our analysis of results by using a base set of parameters (specified in Appendix C) chosen to parallel outcomes roughly consistent with those found in the real world. These constitute the baseline. From this, insights can be gained by examining how results are produced and how changing one or another parameter can affect those results.

Results by Organization Type

The model, as noted, classifies all organizations using three parameters: size, value, and diligence. Size brings costs and benefits. On the one hand, a smaller organization has a smaller attack surface and thus a higher likelihood of keeping its perimeter from being breached. On the other hand, a smaller organization cannot easily benefit from economies of scale in training and tool use. The numbers bear this out. In the base case, the external hardness of a small organization is 89 percent; that is, only 11 percent of organizations have been penetrated. This hardness falls to 71 percent for medium-sized organizations, 36 percent for large organizations, and 5 percent for very large organizations. For the latter, the model supports the truism that CISOs must assume that the attackers are already inside their networks; the smaller organizations still have a shot at ensuring that their networks are under their complete control.

External Hardness

Over time, the permeability of organizations will shift. The number of computers will rise steadily and the number of devices will rise dramatically (the IoT). Conversely, software is expected to get better.[7] Thus, in

---

little security; attackers cannot simply be stopped at the periphery and must be combated internally. This sets the stage for unexpectedly sharp drops in the external hardness of an organization if an organization's hardness crosses the line from where there is enough inherent hardness to merit boosting (through training and BYOD policy) to where there is too little inherent hardness to merit boosting (and so training and BYOD policy are not deemed worthwhile). The resulting external hardness can drop precipitously.

[7]   Any given piece of code tends to get better as vulnerabilities are identified and fixed and as systemic improvements are made under the rising press of concern over cybersecurity. However, there is a countervailing tendency for software to grow more complex and pick up new features, thereby introducing new vulnerabilities. On net, the model assumes that, at this stage of the software industry, the former effect is more powerful.

the base case, the two cancel each other out—but this is largely because the risk shifts from an organization being penetrated because a computer was insecure to its being penetrated because a network-linked device was insecure (the model's base case assumes that the population of devices is growing far faster than the population of computers). In year 0, 80 percent of organizations are penetrated through their computers; ten years later, 70 percent of organizations are penetrated through their devices.

Training

The choice of how much to train users (the model's construction assumes some basic awareness training is ubiquitous even when the training level is zero) depends on both an organization's size and the value of its assets subject to risk from cyberattack.[8] Not surprisingly, the greater the value of assets, the greater the training.[9] Figure 5.1 details the intensity of training in year 0 and year 10 for each type of organization as indicated by its size. Figure 5.2 details the intensity of training in year 0 and year 10 for each type of organization as indicated by the value at risk from cyberattack.

Not surprisingly, in this model, small organizations (which tend to be less penetrable than larger organizations because of their small surface areas) and those with relatively little at stake are unlikely to invest much in training.[10] Large organizations, particularly those with much at stake (and the ability to reap economies of scale), favor training. In year 10, in large part because the value at risk from a cyberattack has grown so much, the largest organizations with a great deal at risk (e.g., major aerospace companies and defense contractors) invest

---

[8]   One can think of training users as comparable in effect to restricting their privileges and/or access to the rest of the organization; both reduce the effective attack surface.

[9]   Again, in the interests of simplification, the many attributes of training—e.g., intensity, quality, reminders—have been boiled down to one parameter.

[10] Furthermore, small organizations are less likely to invest in training because they do not have the resources (money or time) to do so. And, because information technology is outsourced for many small organizations, anything to do with security (including but not limited to training) is generally less of a priority.

Figure 5.1
Training Rises as a Function of Size, Years 0 and 10

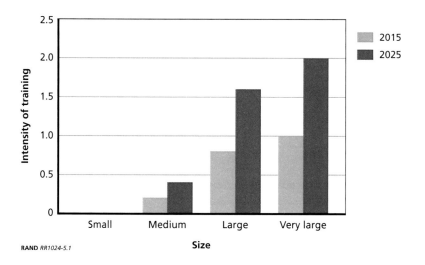

RAND RR1024-5.1

Figure 5.2
Training Rises as a Function of Value at Risk, Years 0 and 10

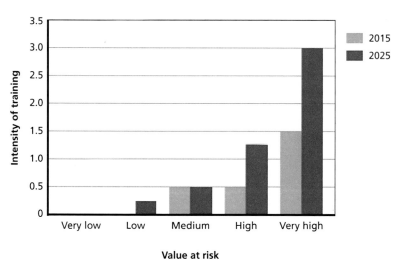

RAND RR1024-5.2

considerably in training (as major aerospace companies and defense contractors, in fact, do).

Tools

The use of tools reflects size (larger companies benefit from scale economies), value at risk, and diligence (the ability to use tools effectively). Over time, tools tend to become more attractive on average because more value is at risk and more tools are available, but half of all the tools used in any one year are subject to countermeasures as hackers adapt if and when such tools become popular. In the model, this adaptation causes tools to lose effectiveness over subsequent years. The charts that follow calculate the total number of tools an organization acquires; it includes those subject and not subject to countermeasures.

Figure 5.3 indicates the average number of tools used as a function of the size of the organization (in years 0 and 10). Figure 5.4 indicates the average number of tools used as a function of value at risk (also in years 0 and 10). Figure 5.5 indicates the average number of tools used as a function of diligence (also in years 0 and 10). Part of the reason diligence appears to be a weak factor is that high-diligence organizations get so much value from the first few tools they purchase that

Figure 5.3
Tool Use Rises Sharply as Size Increases

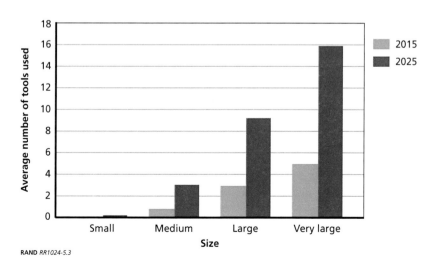

Figure 5.4
Tool Use Also Rises as the Value at Risk Rises

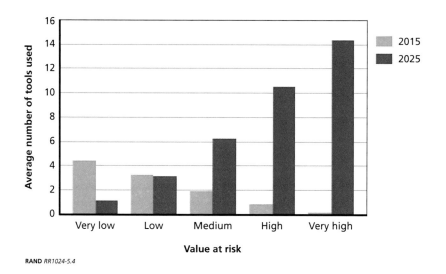

Figure 5.5
Tool Use Is Relatively Insensitive to Diligence

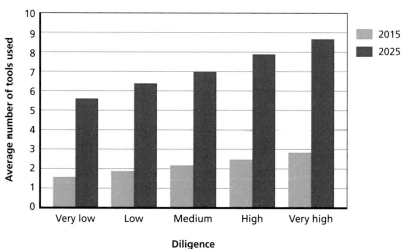

their losses to cyberattack fall quickly—too quickly to get much value from buying more tools, even though high-diligence organizations do use these latter tools more efficiently.

As one might expect from the structure of the model, the efficacy of tools for which countermeasures might exist drifts downward over time. The base average efficacy of a tool is 1.25 percent (the average efficacy is higher because every step increase in diligence above the lowest level raises it by a factor of 1.25). This was the case for tools that had the potential problem of countermeasures, as well as those that did not. However, between the beginning of year 0 and the end of year 10, the efficacy of those tools subject to countermeasures fell by an average of 65 percent.[11]

Device Management

The gain from imposing rules on devices brought into or otherwise present in the workplace rises as the number of noncomputing devices rises—which exceeds the comparable rise in the number of computers (in the model's base case). The *cost-effectiveness* of imposing such rules, however, must assume that there is some value in raising an organization's external hardness by limiting its attack surface. Strict rules on device management might not fit for either a company whose external hardness is very high (by dint of being small and thus having a small attack surface) or one whose external hardness is very low (by dint of being very large and thus connecting so many computers to its networks that one of them is almost certain to have been breached). Finally, although the usefulness of BYOD/smart device policies does not directly depend on the diligence of an organization's use of tools, organizations that have tackled their cybersecurity problems by their adroit use of tools have a correspondingly lower requirement for tough BYOD/smart device policies.[12]

The restrictiveness of BYOD/smart device policies (where the higher the restriction level, the more constraints there are on bringing

---

[11] No graphs in the text describe this relationship.

[12] Part of the reason is that the model has organizations optimize their tool use first and only then optimize their BYOD policies.

devices into the workplace and/or attaching them to the organizational network) in year 0 has

- a complex relationship to size (the very large and medium-sized organizations were at restriction level 1; the large organizations at roughly 1.5; and the smallest at roughly 0.5)
- a strong relationship to value (extra high–value organizations were at restriction level 2; high-value organizations at restriction level 1, average organizations at 0.5; and the rest had few if any restrictions)
- an inverse relationship with diligence (extra high–diligence organizations rarely had restrictions; high-diligence organizations had restrictions half of the time, and the rest averaged a restriction level of 1).

In year 10, as devices proliferate, BYOD/smart device policies impose more restrictions:

- The restriction of BYOD/smart device policies still has a complex relationship to size: very large and medium-sized organizations were at restriction level 3.5, while large organizations were at restriction level 4.5 and the small ones were at 2.5.
- Restriction declines as the value at risk declines (from restriction level 6 for the very high–value organizations, to 4, 2.5, 1, and 0.5 for successively lesser-value organizations).
- Similarly, restriction levels have had to rise as the diligence with which organizations applied tools declined; from 0.5 restriction level for those operating at the highest diligence level to 1.5, 3, 4, and 5 for successively less-diligent organizations.

Air-Gapping

The last technique on an organization's agenda (in this model) is to isolate the most critical parts of an organization's network from the Internet, proportionally reducing how exposed an organization is to loss, but at the risk of losing the benefits from networking.[13] The number of parts (out of 20) of an organization that are worth air-gapping in year 0

- goes up with size (2.5 parts for very large organizations, 1.5 for large ones, 1 for medium-sized, and 0.5 for small ones)
- goes up with value (3 parts for extra high–value organizations, 2 parts for high-value organizations, 1 part, on average, for the next two, and rarely for the extra low–value organizations)
- has no relationship with diligence (1.5 for all classes).

Year 10 results are very similar—perhaps because the increasingly vigorous use of tools moderates the potential losses arising from cyberattacks and hence the relative value of networking.

The Impact on Annual Costs
Figure 5.6 details the annual losses from cyberattacks and the costs associated with using various instruments of protection: training costs, tool costs, the indirect costs (e.g., loss of network access) associated with restricting BYOD/smart devices, and the indirect costs associated with air-gapping parts of an organization. These four cost categories sum to the total cost of efforts to achieve cybersecurity for an individual organization or for all organizations taken together. The topmost value shown (indicated by large dots) is the amount that losses would have been if no cybersecurity instruments had been used. The presentation of the results posits 2015 as year 0. Except where otherwise indicated, figures in this chapter are normalized so that the losses to cyberattack in 2015 (year 0 in the model) are equal to 1. This helps focus on the percentage change in costs over time and the comparison between various cost categories (e.g., the costs of using instruments relative to the losses from cyberattack).

The most important outcome is that the cost of cyberattacks (overall column height) continues to rise (given the model's param-

---

[13] Because the percentage of an organization's value at risk from cyberattacks from the most sensitive segment was generated randomly for every organization type, the correlation between an organization's attributes and its air-gapping policies is not as clear as if that percentage were the same for all organizations regardless of attributes.

Figure 5.6
Base-Case Losses and Instrument Costs for the Model

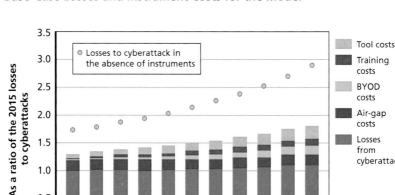

eters) over the next ten years by 38 percent.[14] Most of the increase is accounted for not by the increase in the losses from cyberattacks but from the cost of increasing the efforts to restrain the losses from cyberattacks: e.g., tools, training, restricting BYOD/smart devices, and air-gapping combined. The total column height (including the yellow/gold losses-in-the-absence-of-instruments portion) in Figure 5.6, however, is a reminder that such instruments kept losses from being worse and rising faster.

The growth rates of expenditures in each of these four lines vary by characteristic, particularly by the size of the organization. Table 5.1 shows results for 2015 (year 0) and 2025 (year 10). The smaller companies suffer fewer losses and see no great need to invest in training, tools, or controlling devices, but retain some requirement for selective air-gapping. The larger companies invest heavily in all four categories, especially tools.

---

[14] As a baseline, the average loss per incident in the model is presumed to rise 5 percent annually, or 63 percent over the ten-year period.

Table 5.1
Losses and Costs by Size of Organization (as a ratio of the 2015 losses to cyberattacks)

Size	Year	Losses from Cyberattack (%)	Training Costs (%)	Tool Costs (%)	Implicit Cost of BYOD Policies (%)	Implicit Cost of Air-Gapping (%)
Small	2015	7.80	0.00	0.00	0.08	0.80
	2025	10.25	0.00	0.15	1.60	1.18
Medium	2015	17.92	0.27	0.58	0.33	2.46
	2025	19.85	1.35	3.17	3.74	2.83
Large	2015	32.18	1.89	2.76	0.71	6.05
	2025	32.69	1.28	8.73	6.35	5.63
Very Large	2015	42.10	1.28	3.52	0.27	9.49
	2025	46.84	4.79	11.09	4.99	9.92

Examples of Results

This heuristic model provides a framework for examining the global course of cybersecurity, but, because it is composed of the actions of more than 100 types of organizations, it can also be used to tell a story about each of them. By way of illustration, let us consider three types of organizations:

1. a medical practice: Assume that it is small, has a high value at risk, but has only average diligence in its (potential) use of tools.
2. a defense contractor: Working on specialized unclassified components and is therefore of interest to foreign intelligence agencies. Assume that it is mid-sized but with very high value at risk and assume that it happens to have very high diligence in its (potential) use of tools.
3. a bank: Assume that it is very large, has an average amount of value at risk (relative to its size), but has a high diligence in its (potential) use of tools.

We now look at what kind of choices each makes in selecting instruments (Figure 5.7).

From this figure, it appears that the small medical establishment gets most of its improvement from restricting devices and selective air-gapping, while the bank is a heavy buyer of tools, and the defense manufacturer leans heavily on device restriction as well.

Each of them has a separate story when it comes to its losses over time from cyberattacks. These data are presented in Figure 5.8, which is normalized so that the 2015 (year 0) loss as a result of cyberattacks suffered by the bank is set equal to 1.

Sensitivity Analyses

We now look at how changing some of the variables might change the cost numbers of the model.

Loss per Cyberattack: How would the numbers change if the annual growth rate of the loss per cyberattack were half as fast (2.5 percent)

Figure 5.7
Instrument Choices Made by Different Organizations in 2015 and 2025

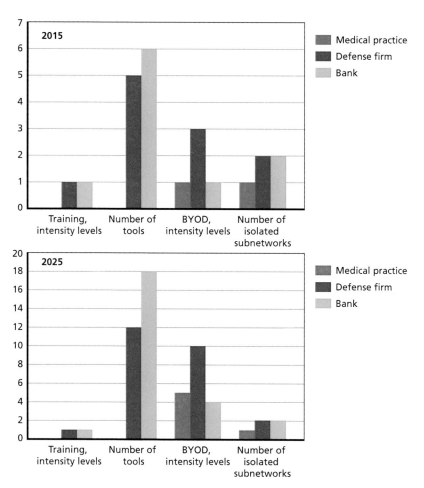

Figure 5.8
Losses Due to Cyberattacks

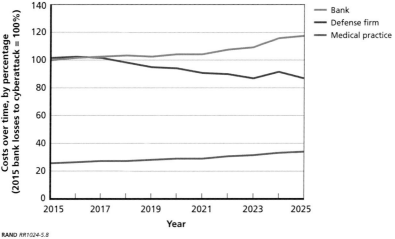

RAND *RR1024-5.8*

or twice as fast (10 percent) as the 5 percent posited in the base case (even as the cost of using the various instruments remains the same as in the base case)? Not surprisingly, the greater the losses per incident, the higher the incentives to invest in such instruments.

Figure 5.9 shows the ratio of various cost parameters (e.g., losses from cyberattack, tool costs) between the high-growth and the low-growth cases. The orange "Losses from Cyberattack" line represents the growth in the average loss from a successful cyberattack; it is meant just for comparison. The fact that organizations do have access to instruments keeps the overall attack costs from rising as fast as the cost per cyberattack (there are fewer successful cyberattacks). But two categories of instruments rise particularly fast: BYOD/smart device policies (they grow much more severe over time), and the amount of training. Both appear to be quite sensitive to prices.[15]

Underlying External Hardness: We also look at the core equations that define how much loss organizations would suffer from cyberat-

---

[15] Alternatively, the wide distribution in the efficacy of tools and of air-gapping policies (thanks to the introduction of random factors in their value) makes them less sensitive to price.

Figure 5.9
Training Is Very Sensitive to Differences in the Growth Rate of the Loss per Cyberattack

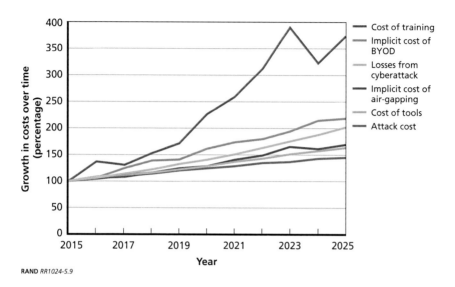

tacks. The seven (user-set) parameters are the annual growth rate of computers, the initial (year 0) ratio of devices to computers, the annual growth rate of devices, the vulnerability of computers, the annual change in that vulnerability, the vulnerability of devices, and the annual change in that vulnerability. Because these variables are exogenous, we look at the annual loss from cyberattacks—before and after all the instruments (training, tools, BYOD/smart device restrictions, and air-gapping) come into play.

Figure 5.10 indicates what happens if every computer and device that could be infected were infected. Given the structure of the model, organizations would have only two instruments with which to play: tools and air-gapping (because training and BYOD/smart device restrictions would not raise external hardness up from 0 as long as the organization had at least one computer or device exposed to the outside world).

In Figure 5.11, we play with the ratio of devices to computers: using 0.25 (devices per computers) to represent "fewer," and 1.0 (devices

Figure 5.10
Both Software Hardness and the Availability of Instruments Are Important to Managing Losses from Cyberattack

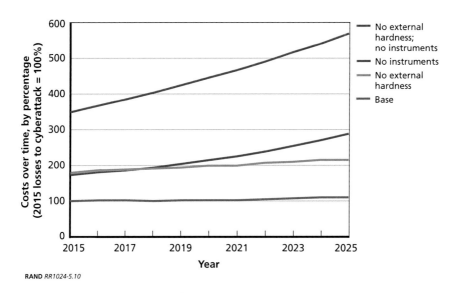

Figure 5.11
The More Smart Devices (Relative to Computers), the Greater the Losses from Cyberattack

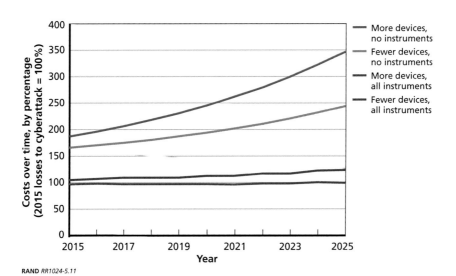

per computers) to represent "more." Shifting the ratio has a significant effect on pre-instrument and post-instrument attack costs (recall, the instruments are tools and air-gapping).

Growth Rate of Computers: We also varied the growth rate in the number of computers in the model, using four alternative rates (Figure 5.12): 2.5 percent (very slow), 5 percent (measured), 10 percent (baseline), and 20 percent (fast). With varied growth rates come varied cost curves. Unlike the case when changing the device/computer ratio, the ability of instruments to moderate the large difference is substantially less (if computer use grows very slowly, pre-instrument losses from cyberattack decline by one-quarter relative to the base case, but post-instrument overall costs drop by one-half).

Growth Rate of Devices: Differences in the annual growth rates of devices—15 percent and 40 percent were modeled (compared with 25 percent in the base case)—are also important (even if the effect is exaggerated because the base-case growth rate for devices, and thus the variations off the base case, are wider than they are for computer

Figure 5.12
Alternative Growth Rates in the Number of Computers Have a Large Impact on Losses from Cyberattack That Persists Even After Instruments Are Used

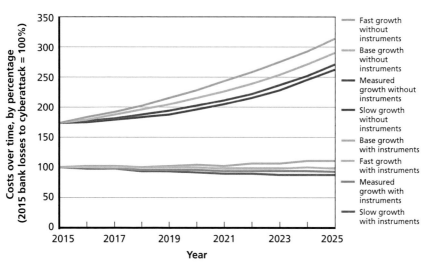

growth). Although the pre-instrument costs vary greatly (a faster growth rate represents a near doubling of costs), the post-instrument cost differences are smaller. The reason is that one of the instruments is to suppress the proliferation of devices (in the model, the population of computers is exogenous). See Figure 5.13.

Substitution of Computers by Devices and Vice Versa: In Figure 5.14, we changed the growth rate of computers and devices together. Instead of the number of computers growing by 10 percent per year and the number of devices growing by 25 percent per year, we examined a range of growth rates. In one run, 5 percent was subtracted from the growth rate of computers and added to the growth rate of smart devices; in the other run, the opposite shift was made. As a general rule, substitution from computers to devices yields a lower set of losses to cyber-attack; this result is achieved, however, because a world of more-available devices is also a world in which organizations optimize to restrict device use more and thus suffer more costs from limiting the usefulness of their networks (the model's parameters reflect the fact that devices are harder to hack into than computers are). The net costs—

Figure 5.13
Alternative Growth Rates in the Number of Devices Have a Large Impact on Losses from Cyberattack, but Instruments Can Sharply Reduce the Difference

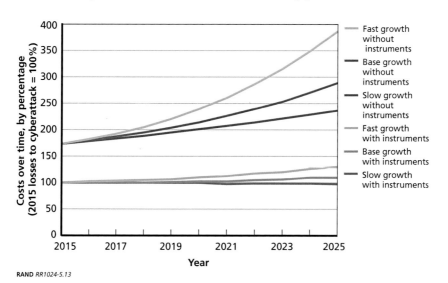

Figure 5.14
Shifting Growth from Computers to Devices Reduces the Losses from Cyberattacks but Only After BYOD/Smart Device Policies Are Taken into Account

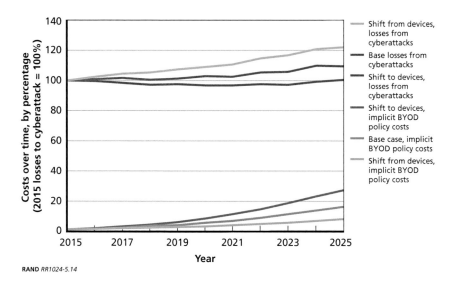

RAND RR1024-5.14

losses plus the cost of implementing security measures—are roughly the same regardless of whether substitution takes place.

Baseline Vulnerability of Computers (but Not Devices): We then examined differences that result in playing with the vulnerability of computers in year 0: "Loose" represented a computer whose odds of being penetrated was twice that of the base case, and "tight" represented one whose odds were half that. This, too, made a huge difference. Indeed, this is one of the few parameters that narrows rather than widens over time. Of greater note was that the cost difference, after instruments were applied, was at least or even larger than the cost difference before instruments were applied. This is illustrated in Figure 5.15.

Growth Rate of Software Improvement in Computers: A similar tale, in Figure 5.16, might be told by varying the rate at which software improves. In the base case, the odds that a single computer can be penetrated are reduced by 15 percent per year; in the test cases, the improvement rate is either twice as fast or twice as slow. Such differ-

Figure 5.15
Baseline Software Vulnerability Makes a Big Difference in Losses from Cyberattack That Instruments Cannot Counteract

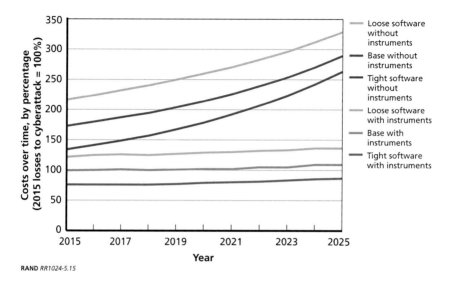

Figure 5.16
Changes in the Improvement Rate of Software Vulnerability Make a Big Difference in Losses from Cyberattack That Instruments Cannot Counteract

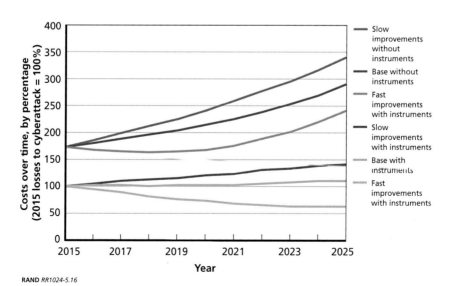

ences initially have a large effect on the (pre-instrument) external hardness of organizations, but, in the longer run, the curves are dominated by the likelihood of penetrating an organization through its noncomputer devices. However, the differences persist when looking at post-instrument external hardness, in large part because one of the instruments, again, is restricting the proliferation of noncomputer devices. Thus, by year 10, the difference between twice as fast and twice as slow is well over 3:1 in terms of the cost of cyberattack. The upper lines represent pre-instrument losses; the lower lines, post-instrument losses.

Baseline Vulnerability of Devices: If the variable to be tinkered with is the vulnerability of devices, the converse story can be told. Figure 5.17 examines a base case, an alternative in which devices were twice as resistant to attack, and an alternative in which devices were half as resistant to attack. The difference expands as the years progress. However, when instruments are factored in, the difference is substantially reduced, again, in large part because one of the policy instruments is the ability to reduce the device count.

Figure 5.17
Baseline Device Vulnerability Makes a Difference to Losses from Cyberattack That Instruments *Can* Counteract

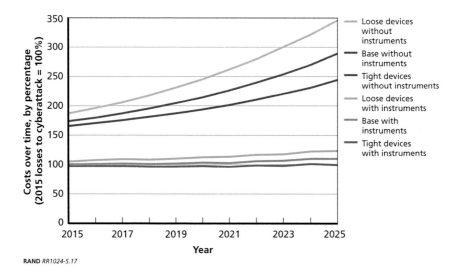

Growth Rate of Software Improvement in Devices: Finally, a similar story emerges if the rate of improvement in device software is charted. Over a ten-year period, software quality makes a great deal of difference before instruments are taken into account—and a significant, albeit attenuated difference, after the instruments are applied. See Figure 5.18.

Training

Training Costs: Figure 5.19 moots training costs that are, alternatively, twice and then half as expensive as in the base case. The more expensive cybersecurity training is, the less that will be purchased, and the greater the losses that can be expected from a cyberattack. Training costs are quite sensitive to the price of training (far more money would be spent on training if the costs were lower, and vice versa). Such training would have a significant effect on the penetrability of computers and hence the external hardness of an organization. Unfortunately, most of the benefit from fewer cyberattacks would be eaten up by the additional cost of training, leaving organizations only somewhat better

Figure 5.18
Changes in the Improvement Rate of Device Vulnerability Make a Big Difference in Losses from Cyberattack That Instruments *Can* Counteract

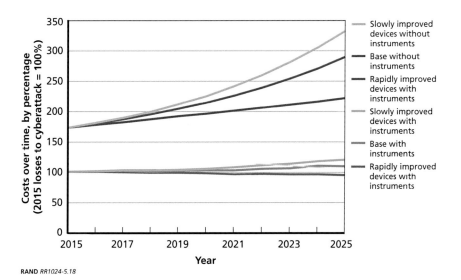

Figure 5.19
Changing the Price of Training Reduces the Losses from Cyberattack but Increases Costs

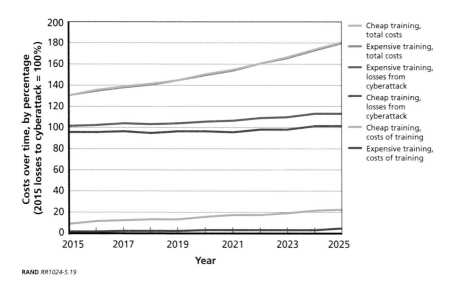

off if the cost of training fell (or only somewhat worse off if the cost of training rose).

Cost of an Increase in Level of Training: In Figure 5.20, we look at the impact of doubling or halving the efficacy of the training tools (measured by how much each level of training reduced the effective number of exposed computers). Improving the efficacy of training has a substantial impact on the losses suffered as a result of cyberattacks. Unfortunately, when factoring in the additional cost of training to take advantage of its increased efficacy (or reduced cost of training if efficacy were lower), most of the difference, again, disappeared. Some of this is an artifact of the model's design, in which training decisions precede decisions to isolate subnetworks. The difference associated with doubling the efficacy of training is far larger than the difference associated with halving the efficacy of training.

Figure 5.20
Changing the Efficacy of Training Reduces Losses from Cyberattack but Increases Costs

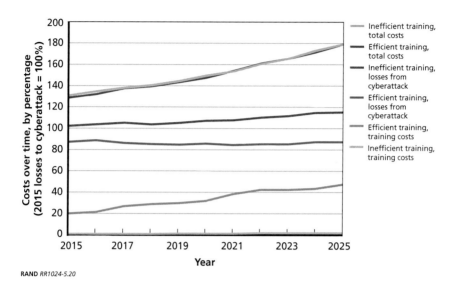

Tools

The Number of Tools Offered per Year: In the base model, two new tools are introduced every year. What happens if four tools are introduced every year? The most direct effect is that an organization would have a larger choice, allowing it to substitute more-effective tools for some of those whose effectiveness was just middling. Overall costs from insecurity in cyberspace would decline. By year 10, the cost of cyberattacks themselves would decline substantially, although half of the savings are eaten up by the cost of buying and operating the new tools required to suppress the growth of cybersecurity costs (offset, in turn, by slight reductions in the cost of imposing restrictions on BYOD/smart device use and connectivity). See Figure 5.21.

The Effectiveness of Tools: In the base model, the underlying effectiveness of a tool is 2.5 percent, meaning that the use of each tool (including those for which countermeasures are effective and those for which countermeasures are not effective and adjusted for its tool rating and for the diligence of the organization) reduces the cost of cyber-

Figure 5.21
Increasing the Number of New Tools Reduces Losses from Cyberattack but Increases Expenditures on Tools Somewhat

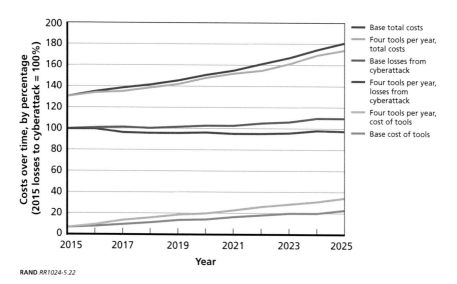

RAND RR1024-5.22

attacks by that much. What happens if the effectiveness of each tool were doubled to 5 percent? This causes a substantial shift in the cost associated with cyberattacks, offset only modestly by an increase in the cost of using more tools, as shown in Figure 5.22. Correspondingly, reducing the effectiveness of tools by half raises the total cost of cyberspace insecurity by raising the losses from attacks significantly, offset somewhat by the fact that fewer tools are purchased.

The Price of Tools: Changing the prices of the tools—doubling them (pricey) or halving them (cheap)—does not seem to have nearly as much *direct* impact as Figure 5.23 shows. Indirectly, the impact of an expensive tool is to force organizations to reduce connectivity (thus incurring implicit costs); the reverse is true if tools are cheap. Organizations spend less money on cheap tools, but their expenses do not rise that much if tools are pricey (in part because fewer are purchased).

The Tool Countermeasurable Parameter: Playing with the countermeasure parameter (Figure 5.24), we see that the decline in the effectiveness of those tools subject to countermeasures makes little differ-

Figure 5.22
The Effectiveness of Tools Has Significant Effects on the Costs and Losses Associated with Cyberattack

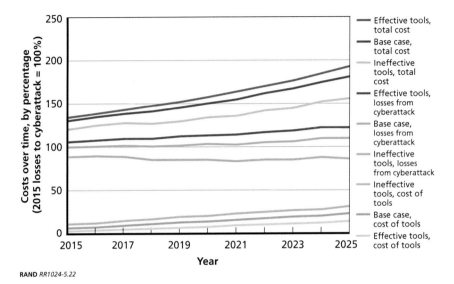

Figure 5.23
Tool Prices Also Have Significant Effects on the Costs and Losses Associated with Cyberattack

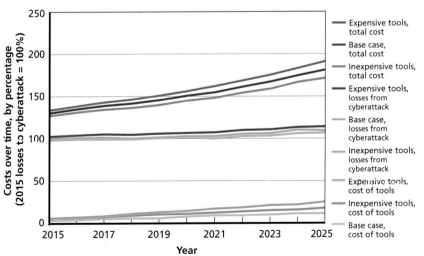

Figure 5.24
Even Weak Countermeasures to Tools Affect Losses from Cyberattack

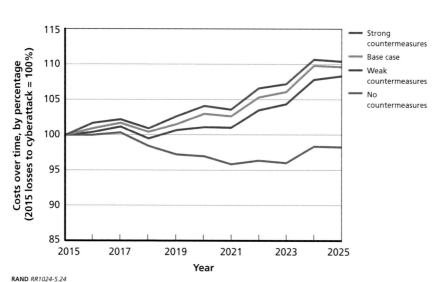

ence. The base case is 75 percent; examining test cases of 50 percent (weak countermeasure effects) and 100 percent (strong countermeasure effects) indicates very little effect on the losses from cyberattack—a difference of no more than 2 percent by the tenth year (even if larger during some intermediate years). This might be because, at even weak rates of countermeasures, nine of the top ten tools available to defenders will be those tools from past years whose value has not decreased as a result of countermeasures.

BYOD/Smart Device Policies and Air-Gapping

Variations in the value of connectivity (from twice to half that of the base case)—hence the cost of wielding such instruments as restrictive BYOD/smart device policies and air-gapping—have a tangible but modest effect on the costs of cybersecurity. It works in the expected direction: The more value from connectivity, the fewer connectivity-blocking instruments merit employment and thus the greater the losses from cyberattacks. The actual cost of restrictions, however, is the same, suggesting that both instruments have a cost elasticity of

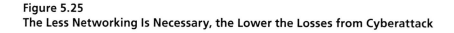

Figure 5.25
The Less Networking Is Necessary, the Lower the Losses from Cyberattack

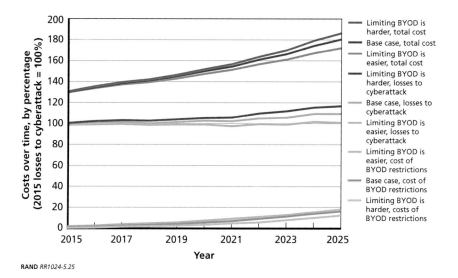

RAND RR1024-5.25

roughly 1 (the number of burdens imposed falls as the cost per burden rises). Figure 5.25 portrays the losses from cyberattacks and the costs of restrictions.

The Efficacy of BYOD/Smart Device Policies: Similar, but stronger, effects arise when looking at the efficacy of BYOD/smart device policies—again doubling (efficient) and halving (inefficient) the ability of each level of severity on the implicit population of devices. Over a ten-year period, there is a substantial improvement in the losses associated with cyberattacks that is somewhat offset by the increased costs of implementing BYOD/smart device policies. Figure 5.26 shows the total cost of cyberinsecurity (the cost of attacks plus the cost of preventions), the losses from cyberattack (alone), and the cost of BYOD/smart device policies.

Air-Gapping: Costs appear to be relatively sensitive to changes in the various parameters associated with air-gapping. Changing (that is, doubling or halving) the factor that converts the degree of air-gapping into a monetary cost (in terms of the lost value from connectivity) has a substantial effect on the losses to cyberattack and retains most

Figure 5.26
How Changing the Efficacy of BYOD Policies Affects the Losses from Cyberattacks with Only Modest Offsetting Costs

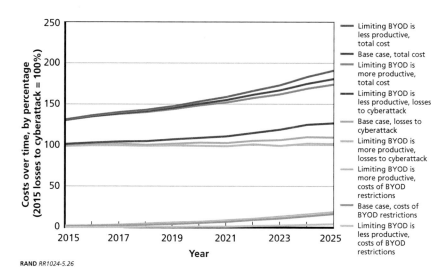

RAND *RR1024-5.26*

Figure 5.27
Total Costs Go Down When Air-Gapping Becomes Cheaper

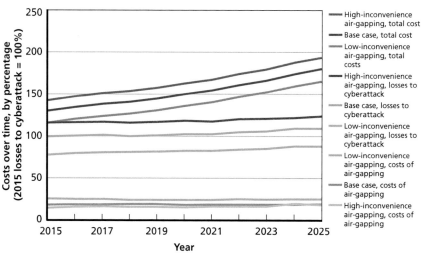

RAND *RR1024-5.27*

of that even after changes in the cost of using instruments has been factored in (see Figure 5.27).

Conclusions

Although the model yields a plethora of results, the following appear worthy of note.

The various instruments that organizations can use to control the losses from cyberattack are collectively powerful. Yet much of what they do is transfer costs from cyberattack losses to the cost of the effort necessary to manage losses; for all model years, roughly 40 percent of the reduced losses are offset by increased costs associated with using such instruments (direct acquisition and usage costs plus implicit reduction in the value of networking). Developing instruments that offer better cost-effectiveness ratios would be useful.

The size of the organization matters greatly to its optimal strategy. Small organizations benefit from circumstances and policies that reduce their attack surfaces (e.g., BYOD/smart device restrictions). Larger organizations need a panoply of instruments to keep costs under control.

Although instruments are important, exogenous factors—notably the quality of software used by organizations—have a very large effect on the losses from cyberattack (and at relatively low cost compared with the cost of cybersecurity tools). There need to be better mechanisms to convey the interests organizations have in the quality of code to those responsible for writing such code.

Over time, the potential influence of smart devices on cybersecurity will approach and perhaps exceed the influence of computers on cybersecurity. The introduction of networked computers into organizations in the 1980s and 1990s was allowed to happen without a very sophisticated understanding of the security implications. It would be useful if the same mistake were not made with smart devices.

The model posits that security implications arising from the growth of the number of smart devices can be managed by policies that limit the connections between smart devices and networks. This is why there are strong cost implications from using alternative parameters (associated with smart devices) before the effect of various instruments are considered, but only modest differences after such instruments are brought to bear. By contrast, strong cost implications that affect computers remain even after instruments are considered.

In the model, the use of some instruments, such as training and BYOD/smart device policies, are sensitive to their relative prices and efficacy; other instruments, such as tools and air-gapping, are less sensitive. This seems to be explained by the homogeneity of training and BYOD/smart devices compared with the heterogeneity of tools (some are more powerful than others) and organizations (for some, their value at risk is concentrated in certain functions; for others, the value at risk is more evenly distributed).

Tools without countermeasures are more powerful in the long run than comparable tools subject to countermeasures. By year 10, of the top dozen tools (out of 30), only one was a tool subject to countermeasures (and that was a tool introduced in the last year of the model). Organizational (and public policy) strategy to improve tools should take such factors into account when making long-term investments in cybersecurity. The basic blocking and tackling of network management would appear to be a priority investment, particularly among larger organizations that need fine-grained understanding of what their networks—and more importantly, the systems hanging on their networks—are doing.

CHAPTER SIX

Lessons for Organizations and Public Policy

By every indication, the risks for cyberspace are persistent, evolving, and growing more worrisome. The good news is that organizations are growing more conscious of the threats and of their own vulnerabilities. Breaches, data leaks, and cyberattacks occupy a greater share of a CEO's business day. This portends the increasing allocation of resources and a greater willingness to institute cybersecurity regimes, even at the cost of inconvenience. That noted, there is a great skepticism that the security industry is about to start handing out silver bullets. Most CISOs express the need for better blocking and tackling rather than a long bomb, in football parlance.

From both an organizational and public policy perspective, an optimal cybersecurity program is one that minimizes the total cost of cyberinsecurity, expressed as the sum of the resources spent on cybersecurity and the losses from a cyberattack. In truth, no one really knows the ideal balance between minimizing the likelihood of attack and the impact of attack. No CISOs we talked to thought they could give us an analytical rationale that justified spending a certain amount and no more. Even though organizations know most of the costs of cybersecurity (but only "most," because it is not easy to put a dollar amount on inconvenience or opportunities forgone because of security restrictions), how many attacks or how much damage they have avoided is far less clear.

An alternative goal for cybersecurity would be to ensure that organizations that are diligent in attending to the security of their network (basic blocking and tackling, so to speak) have no serious reason to fear cyberattack. But at the very least, that goal requires

- operating systems and web browsers that, working together, prevent malware from taking root in computers (notably end-user computers and end-point devices)
- network software that can not only identify everything on the network,[1] it can also determine its security state (including the security state of hosted services)
- a knowledge base of cybersecurity comparable in breadth, depth, and precision to the knowledge base of, say, aviation safety.

None of these exists just yet, even if progress is being made on all three fronts.

Lessons for Organizations

Every organization is different; thus, how they manage cybersecurity will and should differ. Each worries about its own threats. Some are primarily concerned about what an incident will do to their reputations— in part, because they protect the assets of others. Some worry about disruption from groups ranging from hacktivists to hostile countries. Others are anxiously trying to keep their intellectual property from the hands of those with bad intent.

Indeed, these differences suggest the first lesson for organizations seeking to protect themselves: **understand what needs protection, and how badly**. The CISOs we talked to understood as much and have learned to internalize the risk calculus of the various C-suites.[2] Correspondingly, we were continually struck by how the need to protect an organization's reputation justified cybersecurity expenditures.

---

[1]   Because such software presumes that every logical device on the network can speak to such software, achievement of this goal might require not only technology but also some level of standardization, such as universally recognized application portability interfaces (API).

[2]   *C-suite* refers to officials at the corporate levels, such as CEOs and CISOs.

Reputation is not an absolute; it is a matter of perception and exists only relative to expectations and competitors.

From the perspective of global cost minimization, the emphasis on reputation has important second-order effects if corporations are more motivated to reduce the appearance of loss than to reduce actual loss.[3] Consider the summer 2014 attack on JP Morgan Chase. Although more than 80 million accounts were compromised, hackers did little but gather the name, phone number, email address, and physical address of each customer (only somewhat more information than is available in a phone book). As of the end of 2014, there was no indication that any more sensitive information was stolen, much less that any accounts were corrupted or money moved. Yet the company's reputation for protecting customer information has been harmed, even though little of value was taken. JP Morgan Chase is currently spending $250 million per year on cybersecurity and is expected to double its annual expenditures before the decade is out (Son, 2014). The emphasis on reputation would suggest, therefore, that the money would have been better spent minimizing the odds that a hacker could penetrate *any* database, even if the resulting reallocation increased the odds that a hacker who *did* penetrate a database could more easily go on to do real harm.[4] The primary first-order effects are to increase the amount of money spent on cybersecurity and (possibly) cyberinsurance (Bhattarai, 2014), but as the resources available for cybersecurity tighten, the second-order effects of *how* such money is spent might come to matter more.

The second component of self-knowledge is knowing what machines are on the network, running what applications, with what privileges, and with what state of security. The U.S. Department of Defense had difficulties in remediating its classified network (Operation Buckshot Yankee) after it was attacked in late 2008, demonstrating both the importance and difficulty of configuration management.

---

[3] It is not obvious that reputation would be considered important in a world in which most organizations were hacked.

[4] In hindsight, the discovery that attackers penetrated JP Morgan Chase's network thanks to improperly implemented two-factor authentication supports this point even more.

Many of our respondents understood both parts of the equation, but conceded that there was a dearth of products that would answer this need (many products monitored what was flowing between machines, but not what was flowing within them). The nascent IoT is further indication that configuration management products must cover an increasingly heterogeneous base. This creates a business opportunity for firms that can create a unified configuration management system across an organization of arbitrary logic devices *and* a public policy challenge to create the requisite API standards.

Many of our respondents also spoke up in favor of approaches that could reduce the success of phishing attempts against their employees. Training is one such approach, although it must be reapplied periodically to be effective. Even then, although it can reduce the number of compromised users, it cannot alone eliminate compromise, leaving open the question of whether plugging a large percentage of all holes suffices to reduce the risk to organizations appreciably.

Accordingly, the issue of where to concentrate cyberdefenses within an organization—at the perimeters or internally—is becoming a core choice. A large share of all consequential cyberattacks has attackers gaining a persistent presence inside an organization's network when someone opens up a bad attachment or goes to a bad website (gaining privileges on the least-secured corporate server has, of late, become a viable alternative). Weaknesses in client computers then convert code implicit in the ingested material into programs that either execute their own instructions or respond to external (the attacker's) commands. Were these weaknesses absent or difficult to invoke, gaining a foothold would be that much harder. But we are not yet at the point where we can rely on computers (together with other intelligent devices) not being infected; infections must be expected, and thus the defense of organizational assets must have some internal systemic component that detects and characterizes infections so that they can be eradicated. Conversely, the failure to mount any perimeter defense is likely to leave systemic defenses overburdened—and systemic defenses are neither thorough nor fast enough to reliably keep damage below a threshold of acceptable loss.

Organizational choices can, and perhaps should, be influenced by the likelihood of countermeasures to whatever investment is made, notably in systemic defenses. One class of measures aims to detect attack-related anomalies within a system; a related class uses information about specific attackers to detect their presence. Not only does the success of such products assume a tolerably low set of false alarms, but, over time, these measures will beget their own countermeasures. Thus, a measure that differentiates a particular attacker's effect on traffic from everyday traffic is subject to a countermeasure that makes an attacker's own traffic indistinguishable from noise. A measure that isolates incoming traffic to see what it will do to a recipient machine might be outflanked by malware that detects such examination (as one CISO has remarked) or has other ways of postponing its effects. As a general rule, any measure that can be purchased *in toto* by an organization can be purchased by potential attackers (who already routinely test their malware against anti-virus suites to determine whether it can be detected).[5] Such attackers can then generate countermeasures and successively test them. This is not to say such products are useless: Countermeasures have a lag time, and measures are constantly improving (plus, vendors do not necessarily reveal all their tricks up front), and generating countermeasures forces hackers to improve their game (inducing some who cannot keep up to drop out). But the potential for countermeasures forces measures to becoming increasingly complex and thus more expensive, harder to understand, harder to manage, and putatively less reliable.

But for many measures, countermeasures are attenuated or absent. As explained in Chapter Four, the improvement of operating system and browser software creates opportunities for countermeasures; as noted, the advent of ASLR has generated a demand for ROP techniques. But the consensus is that the resistance of the newest software is improving (e.g., as measured by fuzzing cycles required to find holes or the survival of products that can survive hacking competitions

---

[5] Some cybersecurity products require real-time services; a sufficiently scrupulous vendor might be able to detect and deny service to someone whose interest in the product is to develop countermeasures for attackers to use.

untouched) and that attacks that evade the combination of operating system and browsers to penetrate a target require finding less commonly installed software to exploit (and the less common the software, the fewer machines likely to have it and thus be affected by finding a zero-day vulnerability in it). Furthermore, many of the more-prosaic cybersecurity measures, irrespective of their cost-effectiveness, have no countermeasure. (They might have errors, but that is a different issue). They include, as discussed, user training and configuration management, as well as various forms of access controls (e.g., multifactor authentication, role-based access, least-privilege administration) and, where warranted, isolation (e.g., air-gapping).

Lessons for Public Policy

We heard many things from CISOs, but one thing we did not hear was a clarion call, or even a halting whistle, for national governments to do something about the cybersecurity problem.[6] Collectively, CISOs feel there is very little that governments can do directly, and they expressed little interest—exception for some information-sharing—in what governments might do indirectly.[7]

One question that came up is what might be done to discourage hackers by raising the cost of their activities. CISOs clearly have an interest in making it harder for hackers to attack *them*, but that did not translate into making it more difficult for hackers to attack everyone else, apart from cooperating with law enforcement after a cyberattack. They professed no interest in active defense in the sense of hacking back (there was more interest in gaining intelligence to anticipate attacks under the moniker of "active defense").

---

[6]   One respondent wanted the national government to remove impediments to its employer's doing something about the cybersecurity problem.

[7]   We hasten to add that the perspectives of CISO's do not encompass all perspectives. Many cybercrimes (e.g., a compromised credit card) burden individuals over and above what they burden feckless merchants. Legislation to reflect such costs might lead to more globally optimal cybersecurity decisions but would not make a CISO's life easier.

If progress is to be made in cybersecurity, it could come about through the successive reduction in attack modalities (threat vectors). It *can* happen: Starting with the Code Red worm in 2001, and continuing for the following three years, the Internet was convulsed by a series of worms that spread willy-nilly from one machine to the next. Each generation of worms seemed to traverse the Internet faster than its predecessors, until the Internet began to look very fragile, indeed. But one day, the successive waves of self-replicating worms suddenly stopped. The reason was simple: Microsoft released Windows XP Service Pack 2, which fixed a large number of systemic security problems. Several years later, a novel attack vector arose when people became conscious that computers could be infected by inserting an infected USB stick into them. This attack modality was quelled with changes in Microsoft operating systems, leaving some submodalities at issue (e.g., the complex vulnerability that permitted the more-recent versions of Stuxnet to cross the air gap).

The architectural weaknesses that permit client-side attacks are being worked on in ways that suggest that this attack modality might become decreasingly attractive to attackers. True, even success in this endeavor would not lead to perfect cybersecurity (nor could it, until people themselves were perfect)—not least because potentially useful innovations (e.g., the IoT) will create novel attack modalities. But the second-order attack modalities that attackers turn to might be harder to pull off, more difficult to reap gains from, work in fewer cases, and require more sophistication from hackers. Still, the security community would have anticipate what are now second-order attack modalities in anticipation of the day when they become more useful and must be countered (e.g., as first-order attack modalities become more difficult).

Organizations, notably government organizations, want information from corporations in order to characterize the threat—as defined in terms of who is attacking what for which purpose (and, to some extent, with what signatures and modalities). Information-sharing played a relatively small part in the discussions with CISOs. This might be because information-sharing is being asked to solve lesser problems than it should. [8]

We feel that a better perspective is to view information-sharing as an effort to build a common understanding of how systems fail with the intention of preventing such failures, knowing that the conditions arise from the application of malign intelligence (in this instance, our scenario departs from aeronautic safety or medicine, where the threat vectors are constant, or evolve slowly). Organizations ought to be impenetrable, and the conscientious ones have erected multiple interlocking defenses in an effort to make it so; still, failures occur time after time. A community that is prepared to share what went wrong and what could be done better (notwithstanding the human tendency to never admit faults) could collectively educate the world's CISOs (and by proxy, the world's CEOs and organizations as a whole) and promote higher levels of cybersecurity.

In endeavors in which a community must learn about the threats to its members' well-being (e.g., medicine), collective learning is more efficient, thorough, and robust than individual learning. Therein lies a path to building a body of knowledge

By contrast, the current push for information-sharing is focused on sharing threat information, notably threat signatures (or indicators) such as IP addresses, malware hashes, and other attack modalities. This has its place. The Mandiant report (2013), by providing great detail about the signatures of APT1 (aka Unit 61398 of China's People's Liberation Army), essentially closed down that operation for a few months and hobbled it for many months more—until the unit changed its signatures. But it did bounce back and might be much harder to close down a second time. Similarly, the notion that an expensively (and controversially) constructed scheme for sharing signatures represents the acme of government cybersecurity policy,[9] or can even stop cyber-

---

[8] This is reflected in proposed legislation, such as the Cybersecurity Information Sharing Act (S. 2588), whose true importance for cybersecurity has yet to be determined.

[9] President Obama addressed this at the White House Cybersecurity and Consumer Protection Summit (White House, 2013): "There's only one way to defend America from cyberthreats, and that's government and industry working together [and] sharing appropriate information."

attacks efficiently, must presume that (1) a sufficient share of all serious attacks comes from specific hacker groups that carry out attacks spaced out over a period of time, (2) that such groups have a consistent set of signatures they recycle for multiple attacks, (3) that such signatures can be detected (whereas most APT attacks that have been discovered have been there for almost a year or more), and (4) that such signatures do not evolve over time—and would not evolve even if the pace at which signatures were collected and globally shared were to accelerate (as the proponents of such information sharing would hope to see happen). In other words, such a focused approach to information-sharing presupposes that measures (sharing signatures) do not lead to countermeasures (rapidly morphing signatures), even though that is the very phenomenon that has made the traditional anti-virus business model so tentative.

Some Conclusions

The best reason for being optimistic over the future of cybersecurity is the growth in the ranks of those pessimistic about it. Organizations that lacked CISOs a few years ago—or who had them but ignored most of what they said—now have CISOs who know what they are talking about and are listened to. The market for cybersecurity products is burgeoning, even if the prospects for a magic wand or silver bullet are still elusive. Successive versions of mainline software are getting better, even as new species of computing devices are being introduced.

Yet, the journey toward greater cybersecurity must contend with headwinds. One, as noted in a previous RAND report (Ablon, Libicki, and Golay, 2014), was the rise of markets for cybercrime tools that enable people with hacking skills but no serious familiarity with other criminal skills (e.g., converting stolen credit cards into money) to connect with those who do possess such skills and jointly profit from criminal hacking. Another is the potential rise of the IoT and the consequent profusion of addressable devices, which present potential security holes. Conversely, the potential for improving software quality—notably through more secure architectures and better coding practices—might improve cybersecurity's prospects.

Neither challenge is insurmountable. What matters is that those vulnerable to the depredations of cyberattack—and what organization is not?—are now fully engaged in the battle.

Questionnaire

To determine the extent to which CISOs believed that the cybersecurity tools available were adequate to the challenge or if they were on the lookout for something radically different, we developed a 21-item questionnaire and administered it through a series of one-on-one telephone conversations, generally lasting from 45 to 60 minutes.

We want to understand your perceptions, not necessarily the details of your experience.

1. What threats from cyberspace are potentially most damaging to your organization? What threats do you think your industry does not manage well? (e.g., cybercriminals, APT-type actors, hacktivists, cyberterrorists, nation-states, corporate espionage, etc.)
2. Is the loss of intellectual property an important motivating factor for cybersecurity efforts? Is that concern increasing or decreasing for you? Do you think your intellectual property has value on the cyber–black markets?
3. Do you believe your organization is investing enough in cybersecurity? How do you determine what the right amount is or whether what you spend is worthwhile?
4. If you had an additional dollar to spend on cybersecurity, where would you spend it?
5. What cybersecurity problems do you lack a good solution for? What cybersecurity solutions do you find most effective?
6. If you could invent a new approach to cybersecurity (short of a magic wand), what would it accomplish?

7. How are you managing security for BYOD? How do you keep your users from bringing in malware from e-mail or the Web?

8. Does your cloud strategy (if one exists) contribute to (or complicate) your cybersecurity strategy?

9. Have you ever considered isolating all or part of your network from the Internet? If so, which parts?

10. How much time does your CEO spend on cybersecurity?

11. Do you have a formal cybersecurity risk assessment process? Does your organization carry insurance against threats from cyberspace? If so:

    a. What part of your organization evaluates/recommends/buys it? Does the insurance company mandate certain performance standards from you? If so, what standards, and how have they helped/hurt?

12. Do you participate in formal or informal information exchanges with any part of the federal government including but not limited to DHS or NSA? What about with your peers? How much value do you get from these exchanges?

    a. What information do you exchange with your peers?

13. Do you have a formal loss estimation process after you experience a cybersecurity incident?

14. What is your definition/perspective on active defense?

15. How much effort do you spend to understand particular attackers? Which class of attackers (cybercriminals, APT-type, hacktivists, etc.)? Do you believe better intelligence about such attackers could help?

16. Are you satisfied with the range of options you have for cybersecurity, or are you looking for something radically different?

17. Do you believe attackers (malicious hackers, cybercriminals, APT) are outpacing defenders? Do you expect to have the upper hand vis-à-vis malicious hackers two to five years out?

18. Do you believe that businesses are given the right economic incentives to improve security? If not, what incentives would you suggest?

19. Five years out, what percentage of your security solutions will be managed as a service (MSSP, on-premise FW mgt) or delivered as a service (SaaS, e-mail scanning)?

20. Do you prefer to buy your security and other infrastructure such as networking, storage, and servers from the same or different vendors? Why?

21. How big of a concern are zero-day vulnerabilities to your organization? Do you participate in a bug bounty program? If not, why?

Model Specification

This appendix presents a detailed model specification. Appendix C lays out the parameters used in the baseline run.

Model Specification

The model specification includes equations that cover initial external hardness, training, tools, BYOD/smart device policies, and air-gapping; it concludes with housekeeping and reiteration.

Initial External Hardness

The external hardness of an organization is a function of the likelihood that every single machine or device can repel attack. An attacker tries every computer and every device when seeking one place to penetrate the network. The odds of penetrating any one computer or device are independent of each other. Thus, the odds of *repelling* every single attempt is a product of the odds of each computer's and each device's ability to repel an intrusion multiplied together. External hardness is calculated thus:

$$ExternalHardness = softvuln(year) \wedge (dfsize(df) * (computersCAGR \wedge year))$$
$$* devicevuln(year) \wedge ((dfsize(df) * devices * (devicesCAGR \wedge year))$$

where * is multiplication and $\wedge$ is exponentiation.

Softvuln(year) is the average vulnerability of a computer to penetration. Our model assumes that it changes every year (for the better, one hopes). Both the base vulnerability of the average computer and the annual improvement in vulnerability (that is, the reduction in penetrability) are user-set variables.

Dfsize(df) is the number of computers (and, after further calculation, devices) that an organization has. Here, the model makes some compromises. The simplest assumption—that the number of computers (accessible from the outside) is proportional to the number of employees—when applied across organizations ranging from hundreds of employees to hundreds of thousands leads to uninteresting results. It either meant that small organizations were invulnerable or it meant that large organizations were totally vulnerable. It would not be cost-effective in either case to take further measures, such as increasing training or limiting devices. This seemed contrary to fact. Thus, the model assumes that the number of computers and devices does not rise as quickly as the number of employees; the parameter, *dfsizestep*, is the increase in the number of computers with every tenfold increase in the number of employees. One justification for such an approach is that several paths that lead from one penetration to compromising an entire organization—e.g., the tendency to treat colleagues as trusted peers or the access of any one individual to corporate assets—do not work the same way in large organizations as in smaller ones. This could be because larger organizations tend to compartmentalize assets, and the number of individuals anyone knows well enough to trust rarely exceeds a few hundred. Hence the compromise: a pseudo-scale parameter that can be user-set.

DevicesCAGR is the user-set annual growth rate in the number of computers.

Devicevuln() is to devices what *softwarevuln()* is to computers. As a rule, it tends to be higher; that is, devices are more resistant to external penetration. As with *softwarevuln()*, it is user-set, and improves (one hopes) annually at a user-set rate.

Devices is the number of devices an organization has. The year 0 number of devices (for every size-class) is a user-set ratio of the number of devices to the number of computers; hence the repetition of *dfsize(df)* in the equation. The number of devices in later years is a function of the user-set growth rate of devices, *deviceCAGR*. A reasonable expectation is that the growth in the number of intelligent devices will outpace that of computers (Gartner, 2013).

Training

The purpose of training in this model is to reduce the penetrability of an organization by reducing the *effective* number of computers and training at risk from hackers (alternatively, the model could have improved software vulnerability, but this approach seemed less tractable). The equation for hardness thus becomes

$$softvuln(year) \wedge (numcomputers * (tghelp \wedge k))$$
$$* devicevuln(year) \wedge (numdevices * (tghelp \wedge k)).^{[1]}$$

Tghelp is the reduction, per unit of training, in the effective number of computers and devices as a result of additional training: e.g., if training at Level 1 reduces the effective number of computers and devices by, for instance, 20 percent (*tghelp* = 0.8), then training at Level 2 reduces it by 36 percent (1 – 0.8 × 0.8) and training at Level 3 reduces it by 48.8 percent (1– 0.8 × 0.8 × 0.8) and so on.

But if the optimal training level is to be chosen, then the benefits of training have to be offset by the cost of training:

$$k \wedge tghike * tgcostbase / tgfactor(df).$$

The level of training is denoted by *k*. The model presumes that the cost of training rises with by some user-set exponential of the training level (think of this as a way to represent diminishing returns).

Tgcostbase is a user-set constant (measured in millions).

Tgfactor() reflects the tendency for sophisticated training to be less affordable for smaller organizations. This partly reflects economies of

---

[1] Note that *numcomputers* and *numdevices* represent *dfsize(df)* * (*devicesCAGR* ^ *year*) and *dfsize(df)* * *devices* * (*thingCAGR* ^ *year*), respectively. In the model, there was no need to duplicate that calculation; repeating it in the model's description is equally unnecessary.

scale in purchasing training. Also, smaller organizations can less afford to hire separate cybersecurity training specialists or cybersecurity training evaluation specialists. A user-set factor determines cost reductions in training (per capita) as one moves from smaller to larger organizations.

Tools

Every tool purchased improves the internal hardness of an organization against cyberattack. Hardness, in turn, is measured as reduction in the probability of a cyberattack, given that it has been penetrated. It is calculated as the product of the effectiveness of all tools employed to block the effects of cyberattacks; thus, if an organization buys three tools that successively have ratings of 95 percent, 96 percent, and 98 percent (the rating is in terms of what percentage of attacks go through), then its internal hardness is $0.95 \times 0.96 \times 0.98$, or 89.4 percent—which means that 89.4 percent of all penetrations go through to harm the organizations, while 10.6 percent are blocked.

This percentage effectiveness of each tool differs, as follows. First, every potential tool is given a random rating between 0 and 1 that is the same for all customers. Then each rating is multiplied by a user-set constant to determine how much it reduces the probability of a cyberattack (given a penetration). For instance, if the user-set constant is 15 percent and the rating of a tool is 0.6, then the use of the tool would reduce the probability of a cyberattack by 9 percent. However, organizations vary in terms of how much value they can extract from each tool; each increase in diligence levels raises the effectiveness of its tool use by a certain user-set number. Thus, the actual effectiveness equation is the product of (1) a user-set constant, (2) the tool's rating, and (3) the organization's diligence factor. The organization evaluates tools from most to least effective, stopping when the cost of adding a tool exceeds the benefit.[2]

---

[2]   This is, anyway, the ideal. In reality, human decisionmaking is much less systematic.

The cost of a tool varies with the size of the organization. As with training, every step up in size-category means that the cost of a tool (understood, again, per capita) drops by some user-set percentage (this user-set percentage need not be the same as it is for the cost of training). As with training, the cost of tool acquisition can be understood to reflect not only buying but also operating a tool.

The number and efficacy of tools evolves from one year to the next. At year 0, there are a fixed user-set number of tools. Every year sees a user-set increment in the number of tools. Were that the only change, the quality of the best tools could only go up (or at worst, stay the same) from year to year (because some new tools might be better than those already available). However, another feature of the tool set has an opposite effect. Half of the tools are deemed susceptible to countermeasure; the other half are not. Countermeasures arise because attackers change their behavior, tactics, and signatures to vacate the capabilities of certain tools, particularly those that rely on distinguishing the effects of attacks or attackers from normal network and system behavior. The efficacy of *those* tools declines in direct proportion to their popularity (the percentage of organizations who have bought these tools the year before); the decline rate (for tools that everyone buys but which have countermeasures) is user set. Overall, therefore, the average quality of the tools goes down from one year to the next, although the average quality of the top, say, four tools might still rise.

BYOD Policies

Other options are available to organizations to drive the cost of cyber-attacks further down:

- Organizations could restrict the network connection of noncomputer devices (e.g., smart phones, thermostats, and intelligent appliances) by enforcing BYOD policies. This has the effect of reducing the number of devices that offer a foothold into the overall network (also known as attack surface), thereby raising external hardness and lowering the likelihood of a successful cyberattack. But these policies have a cost, notably in reducing the value of networking.

- To calculate the gain from aggressive BYOD policies, the model revises the original equation of external hardness by substituting

$$devicevuln(year) \wedge (numdevices * (tghelp \wedge choosetg) * (byodhelp \wedge k))$$

for

$$devicevuln(year) \wedge (numdevices * (tghelp \wedge choosetg)).$$

In this equation, k represents the severity of the BYOD policy; if there are no restrictions, then $k = 0$. The term *byodhelp* represents the effective reduction in noncomputer devices. The cost of implementing a policy of severity k is:

$$k \wedge byodhike * connectgood * byodfactor.$$

As with *tghike*, *byodhike* represents an exponentiation factor (e.g., costs rise linearly if *byodhike* $= 1$, by the square of k, if *byodhike* $= 2$). *Connectgood* is a proxy for the benefits of networking to an organization. *Byodfactor* represents the extent to which keeping devices off detracts from the value of networking. All three are user-set parameters.

Air-Gapping

The last policy an organization can adopt is to remove portions of its organization from the Internet-accessible network. The operating presumption is that the costs of compromising certain portions might be disproportionate to the costs of compromising others. Thus, it might make sense to isolate machine controls or supervisory control and data acquisition systems from the Internet while retaining Internet connectivity for sales and billing.[3]

To determine when such trade-offs might make sense, the model divides an organization into 20 pieces. Each piece is assigned a random number between 0 and 1. This random number is converted into a value (by mapping the random number into a bell curve and then cubing the result[4]). The pieces are then sorted by value (of keeping them safe from attack), and their values summed to calculate what percentage of an organization's value is made up of the value of its most vulnerable part or parts.[5]

Consider an organization in which the most valuable part has a value of 19, and the other 19 parts have a value of 1. Half the cost of a cyberattack would be the cost of compromising the most valuable part. If that most valuable part were air-gapped, the cost of a cyberattack would be half what it would have been if no part were air-gapped. In general, if the distribution of value in an organization is more skewed for particular pieces, the option of air-gapping those particularly valuable portions becomes more attractive.

Air-gapping has costs represented by the term

$$(k \wedge airgaphike) * connectgood * byodfactor,$$

where k is the number of pieces that are isolated. This equation is analogous to the equation for adopting variously severe BYOD policies

---

[3] In reality, the cost in terms of lost connectivity of isolating certain parts of an organization might also differ among those parts—but this effect can be captured by thinking of the benefit of isolation relative to the cost of doing so, rather than as an absolute.

[4] If the highest of 20 random numbers is 0.98, then the initial value is the 98th percentile of the bell curve, or 2.05, and the final value is 2.05 cubed, or 8.6. So, the value of the most valuable part of the organization is 8.6.

[5] For instance, the most valuable piece of an organization might be a third of the value of the entire organization (e.g., if the value of one chunk is 9.5 and the value of all other chunks is 1, the sum is 28.5, and the 9.5 is a third of 28.5). The total value of any organization is fixed prior to any calculation about the value of each of its parts. Thus, this organization is no more valuable than an organization where all parts have a value of 1. Value is just distributed differently in each organization.

in that *airgaphike*, *byodfactor*, and the aforementioned *connectgood* are all user-set.

Housekeeping and Reiteration

In each of the latter four subroutines—training, tools, BYOD policies, and air-gapping—the organization intensifies its efforts until the costs of going up one more level (or buying one more tool) exceeds the benefit available from reducing expected costs of cyberattack.

Everything else about the model is housekeeping. The costs of cyberattack, the direct costs of training and tools, and the indirect costs of BYOD and air-gapping policies for every organization in the same size-value-diligence class is multiplied by the number of organizations within that class,[6] and then summed. The model is reiterated for every model year starting from year 0 and running for some user-set number of years.

By way of reiteration, Table B.1 lists the five subroutines, how they work, how they affect the cost of cyberattacks suffered, and what sort of costs they impose.

By way of further reiteration, the following parameters might change from one model year to the next by a constant user-set annual factor:

- cost of a successful cyberattack
- number of computers
- vulnerability of each computer *(softvulnCAGR)*
- number of devices
- vulnerability of each device *(devicevulnCAGR)*.

The number of available tools in year 0 is user-set, and this number is incremented every model year by another user-set factor.

---

[6] By way of example, 24 organizations can be characterized as being of the second-largest size-type, the second-greatest value-type, and average (third-greatest) diligence-type. If the typical organization in that class loses $10 million per year to cyberattacks, then the total global loss for all organizations in that class is $240 million.

Table B.1
Five Subroutines and Their Parameters

Condition	External Hardness	Training	Tools	BYOD Policies	Air-Gapping
How they work	Exogenously	Organizational choice	Organizational choice	Organizational choice	Organizational choice
Impact on cyberattack costs	External hardness	External hardness	Internal hardness	External hardness	Value at risk
Costs they impose	None	Direct costs	Direct costs	Indirect costs	Indirect costs

The efficacy of those tools susceptible to countermeasures drops based on the formula described above (the more popular the tool, the more countermeasures are developed, and thus the faster the efficacy of the tool declines), with its own user-set factor.

Here are all the other user-set variables:

- number of years over which the model runs
- baseline cost of a cyberattack
- reduction that a baseline tool brings to internal hardness
- number of parts that an organization is divided into for the purposes of calculating the value of air-gapping *(totalorgparts)*
- cost per tool, and the extent to which unit tool costs go down as size goes up
- cost per training level and the extent to which unit training costs go down as size goes up (exponentiation factor by which training costs rise as training level rises)
- base value of connectivity—converted by two other user-set variables into the cost (lost connectivity) per BYOD level and the cost (lost connectivity) per air-gap level (exponentiation factor by which lost-connectivity costs rise as severity of BYOD level rises; exponentiation factor by which lost-connectivity costs rise as a function of the number of air-gapped portions rises)
- Year 0 vulnerability of computers and of devices *(basesoftvuln; basedevicevuln)*, as well as the ratio of devices to computers
- number of training levels *(tglevels)*, and number of air-gapping levels
- reduction in the effective number of computers and devices for every increase in training levels (reduction in the effective number of devices for every increase in BYOD severity)
- increase in diligence with every step up in diligence level *(diligencestep)*; increase in the value at risk from cyberattack with every step up in the value level *(valuestep)*; increase in the number of computers and devices with every order of magnitude increase in size.

Baseline Parameters

The following are user-set parameters in the base-case model run:

1. Cost parameters:
   - *baseloss* = 50 (the cost to an organization of being successfully attacked)
   - *toolcost* = 20 (the cost of a given tool)
   - *connectgood* = 500 (a parameter that reflects the value of networking to an organization)
   - *tgcostbase* = 100 (the base cost of training at a certain level)
   - *airmultiplier* = 0.03 (the base cost—when multiplied by *connectgood*—of air-gapping one part of an organization)
   - *BYODfactor* = 0.002 (the base cost—when multiplied by *connectgood*—of instituting one level of restriction on connecting devices to the organization's network)

2. Growth parameters:
   - *lossCAGR* = 1.05 (the annual increase in *baseloss*)
   - *computersCAGR* = 1.1 (the annual growth rate in the number of computers within organizations)
   - *devicesCAGR* = 1.25 (the annual increase in the number of devices)
   - *softvulnCAGR* = 0.85 (the annual change in penetrability of a machine exposed to the Internet)
   - *devicevulnCAGR* = 0.9 (the annual change in penetrability of a device exposed to the Internet

3. Effect parameters:
   - *BYODhelp* = 0.9 (equivalent to a 10-percent reduction in the effective number of devices for every level of restriction)
   - *tghelp* = 0.9 (the reduction in the effective number of computers as a result of increasing training levels)
   - *basesoftvuln* = 0.9997 (the year 0 odds that a machine exposed to the Internet will not be infected)
   - *basedevicevuln* = 0.99985 (the year 0 odds that a device exposed to the Internet will not be infected)

4. Step parameters:
   - *diligencestep* = 1.25 (the increase in tool effectiveness for every step increase in an organization's inherent diligence)
   - *valuestep* = 2 (the increase in cost of a successful cyberattack for every step increase in an organization's inherent value at risk)
   - *dfsizestep* = 3 (the effective increase in the number of computers for every step increase in the size of an organization)

5. Intensity cost parameters:
   - *toolhike* = 1.5 (the exponent that measures the cost of a tool as the size of the organization increases by one step)
   - *BYODhike* = 1.75 (the exponent that measures the cost of a subsequent increase in the severity of BYOD rules)
   - *tghike* = 2 (the exponent that measures the cost of a subsequent increase in the level of training)
   - *airgaphike* = 1.5 (the exponent that measures the cost of air-gapping another part of an organization)

6. Tool parameters:
   - *newtool* = 2 (the number of new tools added by vendors every year over and above the ten tools that exist in year 0)
   - *cmtoolvalue* = 0.025 (the baseline improvement of internal hardness for a given tool)
   - *countermeasure* = 0.75 (a parameter that measures the extent to which the efficacy of a tool drops as its adoption spreads)

7. Other parameters:
    – *computerbase* = 100 (the number of computers in an organization for the smallest one)
    – *devices* = 0.5 (the ratio in year 0 of devices to computers).

Bibliography

Ablon, Lillian, Martin C. Libicki, and Andrea A. Golay, *Markets for Cybercrime Tools and Stolen Data: Hackers' Bazaar,* Santa Monica, Calif.: RAND Corporation, RR-610-JNI, 2014. As of October 24, 2014:
http://www.rand.org/pubs/research_reports/RR610.html

Akerlof, George, "The Market for 'Lemons': Quality Uncertainty and the Market Mechanism," *Quarterly Journal of Economics*, Vol. 84, No. 3, August 1970, pp. 488–500.

Anderson, Robert H., and Richard O. Hundley, *The Implications of COTS Vulnerabilities for the DoD and Critical U.S. Infrastructures: What Can/Should the DoD Do?* Santa Monica, Calif.: RAND Corporation, P-8031, 1998. As of March 5, 2015:
http://www.rand.org/pubs/papers/P8031.html

Anderson, Ross, "Security in Open versus Closed Systems—The Dance of Boltzmann, Coase, and Moore," *Open Source Software: Economics, Law and Policy*, IDEI Presentation, Toulouse, France, June 20–21, 2002.

"Aramco Says Cyberattack Was Aimed at Production," *New York Times*, December 9, 2012. As of October 24, 2014:
http://www.nytimes.com/2012/12/10/business/global/saudi-aramco-says-hackers-took-aim-at-its-production.html

Ashton, T. S. *The Industrial Revolution (1760–1830)*, New York: Oxford University Press, 1948.

Avolio, Frederick, "Firewalls and Internet Security," *Internet Protocol Journal*, Vol. 2, No. 2, June 1999. As of April 4, 2014:
http://www.cisco.com/web/about/ac123/ac147/ac174/ac200/about_cisco_ipj_archive_article09186a00800c85ae.html

Barney, Doug, "Repel Cyber Threats the Managed Service Way," *MSP Today*, May 23, 2013. As of April 16, 2014:
http://www.msptoday.com/topics/from-the-experts/articles/339325-repel-cyber-threats-managed-services-way.htm

Bhattarai, Abha, "Cyber-Insurance Becomes Popular Among Smaller, Mid-Size Businesses," *Washington Post*, October 12, 2014. As of October 24, 2014:
http://www.washingtonpost.com/business/capitalbusiness/
cyber-insurance-becomes-popular-among-smaller-mid-size-businesses/
2014/10/11/257e0d28-4e48-11e4-aa5e-7153e466a02d_story.html

Bilge, Leyla, and Tudor Dumitras, "Before We Knew It: An Empirical Study of Zero-Day Attacks in the Real World," *CCS'12*, October 2012. As of October 24, 2014:
http://users.ece.cmu.edu/~tdumitra/public_documents/bilge12_zero_day.pdf

Bizeul, David, Ivan Fontarensky, Ronan Mouchoux, Fabien Perigaud, and Cedric Pernet, "The Eye of the Tiger," *Airbus Defense and Space* cybersecurity blog, July 11, 2014. As of October 24, 2014:
http://blog.cassidiancybersecurity.com/post/2014/07/The-Eye-of-the-Tiger2

Black Hat, "Honey, I'm Home: Hacking Z-Wave Home Automation Systems," video, 2013. As of October 24, 2014:
http://www.securitytube.net/video/8998

Blue, Violet, "Researcher Reveals Backdoor Access in Samsung Printers," *ZDNet*, November 28, 2012. As of October 24, 2014:
http://www.zdnet.com/
researcher-reveals-backdoor-access-in-samsung-printers-7000008013/

Brancik, Kenneth C., "The Computer Forensics and Cybersecurity Governance Model," *Information Systems Control Journal*, Vol. 2, 2003. As of March 18, 2015:
http://www.isaca.org/Journal/archives/2003/Volume-2/Documents/
jpdf032-ComputerForensicsandCybersecurity.pdf

BugCrowd, homepage, undated. As of October 24, 2014:
https://bugcrowd.com/

Chromium, *Pwnium4@CanSecWest2014: Chromium Security Reward Program Official Rules*, 2014. As of October 24, 2014:
http://www.chromium.org/Home/chromium-security/pwnium-4

Cisco, *Cyber Risk Reports*, undated. As of March 6, 2015:
http://tools.cisco.com/security/center/cyberRiskReport.x

Common Weakness Enumeration, "CWE-416: Use After Free," The Mitre Corporation, 2014. As of October 24, 2014:
https://cwe.mitre.org/data/definitions/416.html

Connolly, Byron, "How the CIO Came to Be: The History of Chief Information Officers," *CIO Magazine*, January 24, 2013. As of April 30, 2014:
http://www.cio.com.au/article/451627/
how_cio_came_history_chief_information_officers/

CSIS—*See* Center for Strategic and International Studies.

Cunningham, Andrew, "Apple and IBM Want You to Use an iPhone at Work, Please," *Ars Technica*, July 15, 2014. As of October 24, 2014:
http://arstechnica.com/apple/2014/07/
apple-and-ibm-want-you-to-use-an-iphone-at-work-please/

CWE—*See* Common Weakness Enumeration.

Cyber Security Strategies, *Advanced Persistent Threats and Zero Day Attacks: An Information Security Battlefield; From Static to Dynamic Defense*, presentation, undated. As of March 18, 2015:
http://www.govware.sg/gw10/dl/
01%20Robert%20F%20Lentz%20Singapore%20presentation.pdf

Dalziel, Henry, "Kali Linux Review and a Brief History of the BackTrack Pentesting Distro," *Concise Courses Security* blog, 2013. As of April 10, 2014:
http://www.concise-courses.com/security/kali-linux-review-and-history/

eEye, *eEye Research Report: Working Toward Configuration Best Practices*, Version 1.0, 2011.

Evans, Dave, "The Internet of Things: How the Next Evolution of the Internet Is Changing Everything," *Cisco*, April 2011. As of October 24, 2014:
http://www.cisco.com/web/about/ac79/docs/innov/IoT_IBSG_0411FINAL.pdf

Facebook, *Report Vulnerability*, undated. As of October 24, 2014:
https://www.facebook.com/whitehat

Fielder, Kevin, "Malware Everywhere, Even on Apples," *Kevin Fielder's Blog*, April 9, 2012. As of October 24, 2014:
http://kevinfielder.wordpress.com/2012/04/09/
malware-everywhere-even-on-apples/

Finifter, Matthew, Devdatta Akhawe, and David Wagner, *An Empirical Study of Vulnerability Rewards Programs*, presentation at 22nd USENIX Security Symposium, Washington, D.C., August 14–16, 2013.

Fisher, Dennis, "Software Security Programs May Not Be Worth the Investment for Many Companies," *Threatpost*, February 27, 2013. As of October 24, 2014:
http://threatpost.com/software-security-programs-may-not-be-worth-investment-many-companies-022713/77571

———, "Research Finds No Large Scale Heartbleed Exploit Attempts Before Vulnerability Disclosure," *Threatpost*, September 9, 2014. As of October 24, 2014:
http://threatpost.com/research-finds-no-large-scale-heartbleed-exploit-attempts-before-vulnerabilitydisclosure/108161

Frei, Stefan, *The Known Unknowns*, NSS Labs, 5 December 2013. As of March 9, 2015:
https://www.nsslabs.com/sites/default/files/public-report/files/
The%20Known%20Unknowns_1.pdf

Fung, Brian, "The NSA Hacks Other Countries by Buying Millions of Dollars' Worth of Computer Vulnerabilities," *Washington Post*, August 31, 2013. As of October 24, 2014:
http://www.washingtonpost.com/blogs/the-switch/wp/2013/08/31/the-nsa-hacks-other-countries-by-buying-millions-of-dollars-worth-of-computer-vulnerabilities/

Gallagher, Sean, "New NSA Chief Explains Agency Policy on 'Zero-Day' Exploits to Senate," *Ars Technica*, March 13, 2014. As of October 24, 2014:
http://arstechnica.com/tech-policy/2014/03/
new-nsa-chief-explains-agency-policy-on-zero-day-exploits-to-senate/

Gartner, "Gartner Says the Internet of Things Installed Base Will Grow to 26 Billion Units by 2020," press release, December 12, 2013. As of October 24, 2014:
http://www.gartner.com/newsroom/id/2636073

Geer, Dan, "Cybersecurity as Realpolitik," August 6, 2014. As of December 30, 2014:
http://geer.tinho.net/geer.blackhat.6viii14.txt

Giles, Martin, "Defending the Digital Frontier," *The Economist*, July 12, 2014. As of October 24, 2014:
http://www.economist.com/news/special-report/21606416-companies-markets-and-countries-are-increasingly-under-attack-cyber-criminals

Goodin, Dan, "Extremely Critical Crypto Flaw in iOS May Also Affect Fully Patched Macs," *Ars Technica*, February 22, 2014a. As of October 24, 2014:
http://arstechnica.com/security/2014/02/
extremely-critical-crypto-flaw-in-ios-may-also-affect-fully-patched-macs/

———, "Crypto Weakness in Smart LED Lightbulbs Exposes Wi-Fi Passwords," arstechnica.com, July 7, 2014b. As of October 24, 2014:
http://arstechnica.com/security/2014/07/
crypto-weakness-in-smart-led-lightbulbs-exposes-wi-fi-passwords/

Google, *Google Vulnerability Reward Program (VRP)*, undated. As of October 24, 2014:
http://www.google.com/about/appsecurity/reward-program/

———, *Announcing Project Zero*, July 15, 2014. As of October 24, 2014:
http://googleonlinesecurity.blogspot.com/2014/07/announcing-project-zero.html

Greenberg, Andy, "Meet 'Project Zero,' Google's Secret Team of Bug-Hunting Hackers," *Wired*, July 15, 2014. 2014. As of October 24, 2014:
http://www.wired.com/2014/07/google-project-zero

Gtvhacker, "Hack All the Things: 20 Devices in 45 Minutes," August 9, 2014.

HackerOne, *The Internet Bug Bounty*, undated. As of October 24, 2014:
https://hackerone.com/ibb

Hamming, Richard, *Numerical Methods for Scientists and Engineers*, New York: McGraw-Hill, 1962.

Health Insurance Portability and Accountability Act, enacted August 21, 1996, Pub.L. 104–191, 104th Cong.

Henry, David, "JPMorgan's Dimon Calls Settling Legal Issues 'Nerve-Wracking,'" Reuters, April 9, 2014. As of October 24, 2014:
http://www.reuters.com/article/2014/04/09/
us-jpmorganchase-dimon-idUSBREA3822W20140409

Hewlett-Packard Development Company, Pwn2Own Rules, 2014. As of October 24, 2014:
http://zerodayinitiative.com/Pwn2Own2015Rules.html

Hewlett-Packard and Ponemon Institute, *Cost of Cyber Crime Study Report*, 2013. As of March 6, 2015:
http://www.hpenterprisesecurity.com/
ponemon-2013-cost-of-cyber-crime-study-reports

Hoffman, Patricia, assistant secretary, Office of Electricity Delivery and Energy Reliability, *Electricity Subsector Cybersecurity Capability Maturity Model (ES-C2M2)*, May 2012. As of March 6, 2015:
https://www.naseo.org/Data/Sites/1/documents/committees/energysecurity/
webinars/2013-03-05/hoffman-c2m2.pdf

Industrial Control Systems Cyber Emergency Response Team, "Incident Response Activity," *ICS-CERT Monitor*, 2013. As of March 6, 2015:
http://ics-cert.us-cert.gov/sites/default/files/
ICS-CERT_Monitor_April-June2013.pdf

Industrial Cyber Security, *Services*, undated. As of March 6, 2015:
http://www.industrialcybersec.com/services.html

Lancope and Ponemon Institute, *Cyber Security Incident Response: Are We as Prepared as We Think?* January 2014. As of March 6, 2015:
http://www.lancope.com/resources/industry-report/
ponemon-institute-report-cyber-security-incident-response-are-we-prepared

Libicki, Martin C., Edward Balkovich, Brian A. Jackson, Rena Rudavsky, and Katharine Watkins Webb, *Influences on the Adoption of Multifactor Authentication*, Santa Monica, Calif.: RAND Corporation, TR-937-NIST, 2011. As of March 5, 2015:
http://www.rand.org/pubs/technical_reports/TR937.html

Lockheed Martin, "Cyber Kill Chain®," 2014. As of October 24, 2014:
http://www.lockheedmartin.com/us/what-we-do/information-technology/
cyber-security/cyber-kill-chain.html

Mandiant, *Intelligence Center Report, APT1: Exposing One of China's Cyber Espionage Units*, 2013. As of March 6, 2015:
http://intelreport.mandiant.com/

McAfee, *Cyber-Security: The Vexed Question of Global Rules, Security Defense Agenda*, February 2012. As of March 6, 2015:
http://www.mcafee.com/au/resources/reports/rp-sda-cyber-security.pdf

———, *The Economic Impact of Cybercrime and Cyber Espionage*, Center for Strategic and International Studies, July 2013. As of March 6, 2015:
http://www.mcafee.com/us/resources/reports/rp-economic-impact-cybercrime.pdf

McConnell, Steve, *Code Complete: A Practical Handbook of Software Construction*, 2nd ed., Redmond, Wash.: Microsoft Press, 2004.

Microsoft, *Microsoft Security Intelligence Report (MSIR)*, Vol. 15, January–June 2013. As of October 24, 2014:
http://download.microsoft.com/download/5/0/3/
50310CCE-8AF5-4FB4-83E2-03F1DA92F33C/
Microsoft_Security_Intelligence_Report_Volume_15_English.pdf

———, *Microsoft Bounty Programs*, 2014a. As of October 24, 2014:
http://technet.microsoft.com/en-us/security/dn425036

———, *Public and Private Symbols*, 2014b. As of October 24, 2014:
http://msdn.microsoft.com/en-us/library/ff553493.aspx

———, *Security Development Lifecycle*, 2014c. As of October 24, 2014:
https://www.microsoft.com/security/sdl/default.aspx

Mimoso, Michael, "Vupen Cashes in Four Times at Pwn2Own," *Threatpost*, March 12, 2014. As of October 24, 2014:
http://threatpost.com/vupen-cashes-in-four-times-at-pwn2own/104754

Mozilla, *Bug Bounty Program*, undated. As of October 24, 2014:
https://www.mozilla.org/security/bug-bounty.html

Naraine, Ryan, "Teenager Hacks Google Chrome with Three Zero-Day Vulnerabilities," *ZDNet*, March 9, 2012. As of October 24, 2014:
http://www.zdnet.com/blog/security/
teenager-hacks-google-chrome-with-three-0day-vulnerabilities/10649

National Institute on Standards and Technology, "Developing a Framework to Improve Critical Infrastructure Cybersecurity," *Federal Register*, Vol. 78, February 26, 2013, p. 13024. As of March 6, 2015:
https://federalregister.gov/articles/a/2013-04413

National Research Council, *Trust in Cyberspace*, Fred B. Schneider, ed., Washington, D.C.: National Academies Press, 1999.

————, *Technology, Policy, Law, and Ethics Regarding U.S. Acquisition and Use of Cyberattack Capabilities*, William A. Owens, Kenneth W. Dam, Herbert S. Lin, eds., Washington, D.C.: The National Academies Press, 2009.

NRC—*See* National Research Council.

NV, "End of the Road for Windows XP," *The Economist*, April 8, 2014. As of October 24, 2014:
http://www.economist.com/blogs/babbage/2014/04/difference-engine

Okhravi, Hamed, and David Nicol, "Evaluation of Patch Management Strategies," *International Journal of Computational Intelligence: Theory and Practice*, Vol. 3, No. 2, December 2008.

Ozment, Andy, and Stuart E. Schechter, *Milk or Wine: Does Software Security Improve with Age?* Proceedings from 15th USENIX Security Symposium, Vancouver, B.C.: July 31–August 4, 2006, pp. 93–104.

Perlroth, Nicole, and Quentin Hardy, "Bank Hacking Was the Work of Iranians, Officials Say," *New York Times*, January 8, 2013. As of October 24, 2014:
http://www.nytimes.com/2013/01/09/technology/
online-banking-attacks-were-work-of-iran-us-officials-say.html?_r=0

Ponemon Institute, *2013 Cost of Data Breach Study: Global Analysis*, May 2013a. As of March 3, 2015:
https://www4.symantec.com/mktginfo/whitepaper/053013_GL_NA_WP_
Ponemon-2013-Cost-of-a-Data-Breach-Report_daiNA_cta72382.pdf

————, *2013 eCommerce Cyber Crime Report: Safeguarding Brand and Revenue This Holiday Season*, RSA Security, October 2013b. As of March 6, 2015:
http://www.emc.com/collateral/analyst-reports/
h12493-ar-2013-ecommerce-cyber-crime-report.pdf

PricewaterhouseCoopers, *Annual Information Security Survey*, 2012. As of June 16, 2012:
http://www.pwc.com/gx/en/information-security-survey

Red Tiger Security, *SCADA Security Maturity Model*, undated. As of March 18, 2015:
http://redtigersecurity.com/services/scadaics-security-consulting/
scada-security-maturity-model/

Reece, Alex, "Introduction to Return Oriented Programming (ROP)," *codearcana*, May 28, 2013. As of October 24, 2014:
https://github.com/awreece/codearcana/blob/master/content/security/
rop_tutorial.md

Rescorla, Eric, "Is Finding Security Holes a Good Idea?" *RTFM*, February 7, 2005. As of December 30, 2014:
http://www.rtfm.com/bugrate.pdf

Riley, Michael, Ben Elgin, Dune Lawrence, and Carol Matlack, "Missed Alarms and 40 Million Stolen Credit Card Numbers: How Target Blew It," *Businessweek*, March 13, 2014. As of October 24, 2014:
http://www.businessweek.com/articles/2014-03-13/
target-missed-alarms-in-epic-hack-of-credit-card-data

Roberts, Paul, "UK's Top Ecrime Investigator Describes a Life Fighting Cybercrime," *naked security*, September 25, 2012. As of April 14, 2014:
https://nakedsecurity.sophos.com/2012/09/25/interview-bob-burls/

Rosenblatt, Seth, "All Hacking Eyes on the Prize Money at CanSecWest," cnet.com, March 13, 2014. As of October 24, 2014:
http://www.cnet.com/news/all-hacking-eyes-on-the-prize-money-at-cansecwest/

S. 2588—*See* U.S. Senate.

Sang-Hun, Choe, "Computer Networks in South Korea Are Paralyzed in Cyberattacks," *New York Times*, March 20, 2013. As of October 24, 2014:
http://www.nytimes.com/2013/03/21/world/asia/
south-korea-computer-network-crashes.html

Schneier, Bruce, "Should U.S. Hackers Fix Cybersecurity Holes or Exploit Them?" *The Atlantic*, May 19, 2014. As of December 30, 2014:
http://www.theatlantic.com/technology/archive/2014/05/
should-hackers-fix-cybersecurity-holes-or-exploit-them/371197/

Shape Security, homepage, undated. As of March 5, 2015:
https://www.shapesecurity.com/technology/

———, *Real-Time Polymorphism: A New Category of Advanced Security Defenses*, undated. As of June 18, 2014:
https://www.shapesecurity.com/assets/downloads/real-time-polymorphism.pdf

Son, Hugh, "Dimon Sees Cyber-Security Spending Doubling After Hack," *Bloomberg Business*, October 10, 2014. As of April 8, 2015:
http://www.bloomberg.com/news/articles/2014-10-10/
dimon-sees-jpmorgan-doubling-250-million-cyber-security-budget

Surfwatch Labs, *Trends in Cybercrime: A Social Look at the First Half of 2014*, SurfWatch Labs report, January–June 2014.

TippingPoint, *Zero Day Initiative*, undated. As of October 24, 2014:
http://www.zerodayinitiative.com/

U.S. Senate, Cybersecurity Information Sharing Act (S. 2588), 113th Cong., 2nd sess., 2014. As of March 6, 2015:
https://www.feinstein.senate.gov/public/index.cfm/files/
serve/?File_id=08de1c1b-446b-478c-84a8-0c3f35963216

Verisign, *Cyber Security, Improved Security Operations and Internet Infrastructure Protection*, 2014. As of October 24, 2014:
http://www.verisigninc.com/en_US/cyber-security/index.xhtml

Verizon, *Data Breach Investigations Report*, April 2014. As of March 6, 2015:
http://www.verizonenterprise.com/DBIR/2014/

Ware, Willis H., *Security and Privacy in Computer Systems*, Santa Monica, Calif.: RAND Corporation, P-3544, 1967. As of March 5, 2015:
http://www.rand.org/pubs/papers/P3544.html

White House, "Summit on Cybersecurity and Consumer Protection," February 13, 2015. As of March 18, 2015:
https://www.whitehouse.gov/issues/foreign-policy/cybersecurity/summit